Microsoft

Access 2013 Plain & Simple

Andrew Couch

Published with the authorization of Microsoft Corporation by:
O'Reilly Media, Inc.
1005 Gravenstein Highway North
Sebastopol, California 95472

ISBN: 978-0-7356-6944-4

1 2 3 4 5 6 7 8 9 TI 8 7 6 5 4 3

Printed and bound in Canada.

Microsoft Press books are available through booksellers and distributors worldwide. If you need support related to this book, email Microsoft Press Book Support at mspinput@microsoft.com. Please tell us what you think of this book at *http://www.microsoft.com/learning/booksurvey*.

Acquisitions and Developmental Editor: Kenyon Brown
Production Editor: Melanie Yarbrough
Editorial Production: Holly Bauer
Technical Reviewer: Andrew Vickers
Copyeditor: Richard Carey
Indexer: Bob Pfahler
Cover Design: Twist Creative • Seattle
Cover Composition: Zyg Group, LLC
Illustrator: S4Carlisle Publishing Services

This book is dedicated to my Mum and Dad, who supported me through all my studies, never questioning what I would end up doing, and gently helped me to achieve several academic goals.

Contents

5 Working with data in datasheets 71

10 Preparing data to print using reports **175**

About this book

1

This book provides a quick reference to specific techniques for working with Microsoft Access 2013 and guides you with clear pictures that you can easily follow to replicate the procedures described. Although the book is designed to be used without sample databases, enabling you to dip into each method without having progressed through previous steps, it does provide links from which you can download samples with the same dataset I have used to help you more closely follow the examples.

Access 2013 is a real treat for those wanting to access and work cooperatively on their data from different geographical locations, while still maintaining all the standard desktop capabilities for developing a local solution to complex business problems.

The challenge for Microsoft has been to deliver a product that can adapt to new technologies, such as the sharing of data through a browser interface, while maintaining a familiar desktop experience for development that embraces the spirit of Access.

What's new in Access 2013?

Access 2013 is a revolutionary step forward, and the challenge in this book has been to offer you a fresh look at the desktop database (because that part of Access has not changed in this version), while also introducing you to the new Web App.

In writing the book, I decided to offer you the new Web App experience in the first two chapters, because when you start Access, the default choice is to create a database using a Web App.

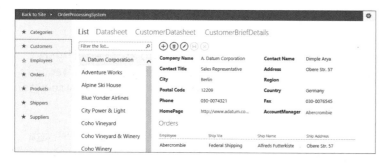

For many years, Access users have been looking for a way to get their databases onto the web, and although Access has gone through several supportive technologies, such as Data Access Pages and, in Access 2010, Web Databases, this has only now matured to a point where we can see a great path ahead. It is my pleasure to give you the first glimpse of what this new technology promises.

A Web App is hosted either in a Microsoft Office 365 Plan (which includes Office 2013 Professional) or in your organization's Microsoft SharePoint 2013 Server running Access

Services, so to work through those sections in the book, you will need this facility. If you are unable to get involved with moving your database to the web, I am sure that many of the other topics will provide a stimulating and fresh look at Access.

When getting started in developing a Web App, you can either take advantage of built-in table templates or import existing data from familiar data sources.

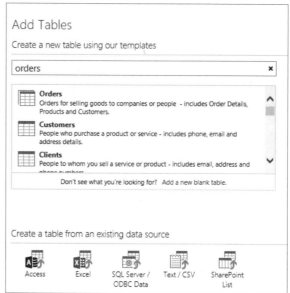

A Web App addresses several important problems when it comes to developing a browser-based interface. The first problem is getting started, and here Access will create for you at least two browser views of your data for each table. The first is a list view, which displays a searchable list of

records linked to areas that then display both the detailed contents of the records and any related records. A Web App has a wonderfully natural drill-down capability to take you to related data. The second view is the datasheet. Access will automatically create one for you, and you can then add more datasheets for a table to provide additional views of your data. You will notice that I use the term *view*. You can think of a view as being the same as a form in desktop database technology.

When you edit data in a Web App Datasheet view, you will have the same desktop experience of interacting with a list of data records on the desktop. However, when you work with other views, you will use the new Action Bar to edit and save your changes.

Other great new features in a Web App are the ability to summarize data, and the Web App's ability to automatically provide a vertical table selector and horizontal view selector for navigating your data.

When you save data in a Web App on Office 365, the data behind the scenes is saved inside a SQL Azure database in the cloud, so you can exploit all the scalable technologies of the very latest in Microsoft online storage.

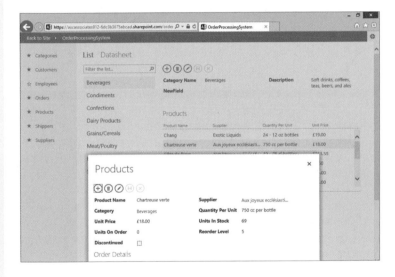

Another key feature of a Web App is that when you need a drop-down list of choices, Access traditionally uses combo or list boxes, but these are very inefficient to use in a browser. The new AutoComplete control allows you to type information and then uses pattern matching to show a reduced list of related choices.

The following older features in Access have been removed from the latest version:

- Access Data Projects (ADP)
- Pivot charts and pivot tables
- Replication
- Upsizing Wizard
- Source code control
- Support for Access 97 databases

A quick overview

Microsoft Access 2013 Plain & Simple is divided into sections, and each section has a specific focus with related tasks. To help you understand how to move around and use the book, I'll now provide a quick overview of the book's structure.

Section 2, "Creating a custom Web App," introduces the idea of creating a Web App and navigating around the key components in the interface. Here you will see how the productivity of the desktop is transferred into creating a browser-based interface for your application.

In Section 3, "Modifying a Web App," we delve a bit deeper under the hood and see how you can add to a custom Web App to create your own views of data, create queries, and use other techniques.

In Section 4, "Creating a desktop database," we look at how to create a desktop database, and we cover creating tables and relationships, which are key to understanding best practices when building a database.

In Section 5, "Working with data in datasheets" (datasheets are an often overlooked feature in Access), I provide a wide range of techniques for getting the most out of your datasheets.

In Section 6, "Selecting data using queries," you'll discover how queries lie at the heart of relational databases. They allow you to bring data together from tables and exploit calculations, parameterization, and many other features.

In Section 7, "Modifying data using queries," I demonstrate both simple and more complicated updates to your data. Action queries offer you features that allow you to perform bulk updates on data.

In Section 8, "Improving presentations with forms," we will explore a landscape of many more advanced presentation features. Forms also allow you to integrate and extend basic datasheet presentation features.

Section 11, "Exchanging data," shows how Access allows you to both import and export data. For many applications, the ability to link dynamically to data in other systems makes Access a number-one choice for bringing together data from different systems and reporting on it.

In Section 12, "Introducing the power of macros," you will discover a unique approach to automating operations and providing more sophistication to your application. In this section, I get you started with several key examples.

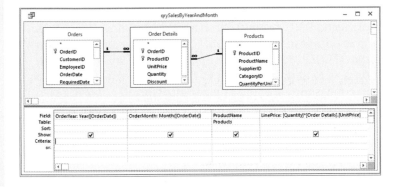

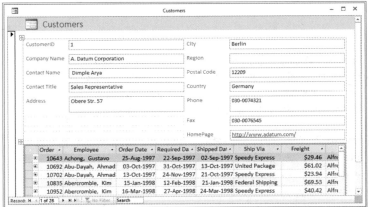

In Section 9, "Using controls effectively," you will enhance your forms and get an understanding of the wealth of controls available in Access.

In Section 10, "Preparing data to print using reports," you will discover a fantastically rich reporting tool, which will allow you to create everything from a simple data list to a complex invoice and then print the results.

In Section 13, "Administrating a database," we look at maintaining your database in good health and securing your data, together with a quick look at tools for improving the design of your database.

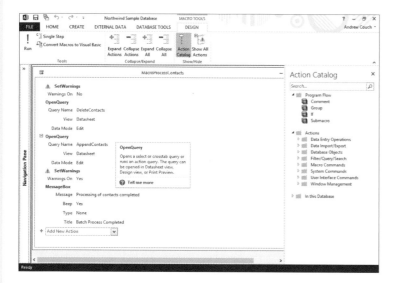

A few assumptions

In writing any book, authors must make a few assumptions about their readers. I assume that you are basically computer literate, meaning that you have used a computer before and know how to turn it on and power it off, how to use a mouse, and how to select text and objects. I also assume that you have worked with some kind of software before and know what a menu, dialog box, and tool button are. I do not assume that you have used a touch screen before because these are a relatively recent addition to computers.

I assume you either use computers at work or at home or both, that you have access to an Internet connection, and you have gone online at some time or other using one browser or another. Other than that, I try to give you all the steps you need to get things done in an easy-to-understand way, regardless of your technical background.

About the sample database

The tasks and procedures in the book use a sample database, provided by Microsoft Corporation, called the Desktop Northwind 2007 sample database. You can download a copy of this database from *http://office.microsoft.com/en-us/templates/TC012289971033.aspx?pid=CT101428651033* to get a dataset that is very similar to the one used in the book, or you can visit my website at *www.ascassociates.biz/Access-2013PandSExamples.aspx*, where you'll find the database and completed examples.

Adapting task procedures for touchscreens

In this book, I provide instructions based on traditional keyboard and mouse input methods. If you're using Access on a touch-enabled device, you might be giving commands by tapping with your finger or with a stylus. If so, substitute a tapping action whenever I instruct you to click a user interface element. Also note that when I ask you to enter information in Access, you can do so by typing on a keyboard, by tapping in the entry field under discussion to display and use the on-screen keyboard, or even by speaking aloud, depending on your computer setup and your personal preferences.

A final word

Access 2013 is preparing the road ahead for productivity in deploying data to be shared over the web. I hope you will share my enthusiasm both for the new technology features in the product and for the solid approach to developing solutions on the desktop.

Creating a custom Web App

2

When you start Access, the first option you see is to create a custom Web App. This new type of application is hosted within SharePoint. It could be installed on-premise with your own company's software, or you could choose to use Office 365.

With a Web App, you get the familiarity of working in the Access environment although the Web App is hosted either in a Microsoft Office 365 Plan (which includes Office 2013 Professional) or in your organization's Microsoft SharePoint 2013 Server running Access Services, so you are creating an app that can be viewed in a browser without Access being installed on the machine. This section contains a number of key activities that you will perform in creating a custom Web App. You will need Access to design and modify your site, but other users can interact with the app using only their web browser.

Because the Web App is a brand-new feature in Access, this section will guide you through creating a Web App, while Section 3, "Modifying a Web App," provides more information on further developing your Web App.

In this section:

- Starting Access
- Creating a custom Web App
- Adding a table template
- Showing the navigation pane
- Adding a blank table
- Launching a Web App
- Working with the List view
- Working with the Datasheet view
- Working with a summary view
- Finding your site and navigating to the team site
- Creating a Web App using a template

Starting Access

On the Windows desktop, scrolling to the right reveals the Office 2013 products that you have installed on the machine. When you start an application, the application opens on the desktop.

If you are using an older version of Windows, such as Windows 7, click the Start button on the taskbar, and then click All Programs | Microsoft Office | Access 2013.

Start Access

1 On the desktop, scroll to the right.

2 Click Access 2013.

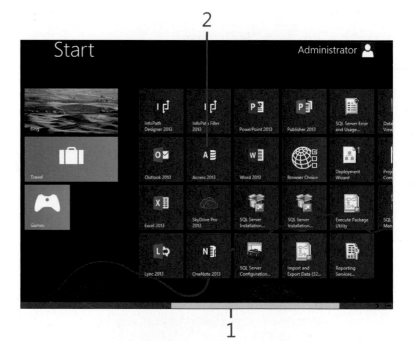

TIP When working on the desktop, if you point to the lower-left of your screen on the taskbar and click the miniaturized desktop Tile, you will quickly return to the Windows desktop, where you can start other applications.

Creating a custom Web App

Access 2013 allows you to create both desktop-based and Web App–based applications. The default choice is to create a custom Web App. In this section, we guide you through the steps to get you started with your first web application.

If you have subscribed to Office 365, you have obtained a domain name as part of setting up your account—for example, *mydomain*. You will use that domain name when typing a web location to create an Access Web App—for example, *https://mydomain.sharepoint.com*.

Create a custom Web App

1 After starting Access, choose the Custom Web App.

2 Type the application name in the App Name text box.

3 Type the URL for your Office 365 domain in the Web Location text box, or select your Team Site from the Available Locations list.

4 Click Create.

5 Sign in to your account. You can also select the Keep Me Signed In check box, which will keep you signed in; otherwise, you will be prompted again to sign in later when launching the Web App.

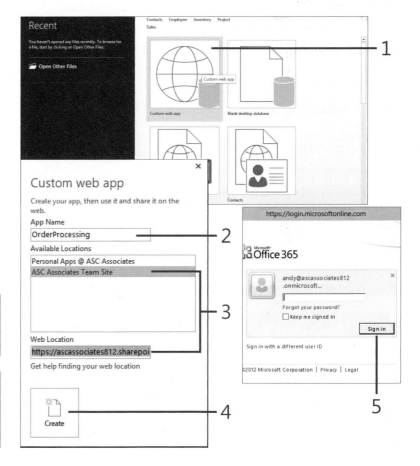

TIP You might already see a list of available locations. If you see any locations referring to Team Site, you can use these as an alternative to typing the URL by selecting the location name.

CAUTION If you cannot get to this point, remember that you need to create the appropriate Office 365 account before you can use this new feature. Otherwise, when you enter your details, you will not reach step 5.

Adding a table template

When choosing a table template, you can type a noun representing the kind of data that you need to store. Access then attempts to match this with one of a large number of common designs.

After a noun is matched and selected, one or more tables are added to your application. This is an extremely powerful way to get started because in addition to simply adding the tables, Access creates a set of views for interacting with the data and creates a menu system for navigating between the views.

Add a table template

1 Type a name for your table, and click the search symbol to see the matches displayed.

2 Select a table from the available list.

3 Click a table in the Table Selector to display a list of available views for the table.

4 Click any item in the View Selector to display the associated view.

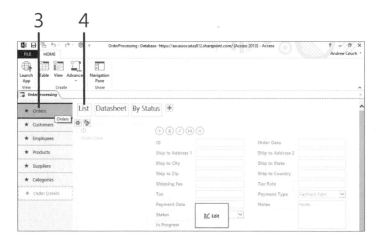

> ✓ **TIP** Typing All and clicking the search symbol displays a list of all available templates. Take care as you scroll through the list because it is easy to click a table by mistake and thus unintentionally create the table. You will also find that sometimes when you select one table—for example, Orders—several other related tables are automatically created to assist you in building the database.

> ⚠ **CAUTION** The term *view* can be a bit confusing if you are familiar with SQL Server. In Access client terminology, *view* has the same meaning as *form*, and a *query* is equivalent to a SQL Server *view*. When you create a table template, Access will automatically generate at least two, and sometimes three, views (depending on the table). You will also find that lookups to link together your views have been automatically added to the selected tables, depending on the tables that have been created.

Showing the navigation pane

Similar to a desktop database application, a Web App provides a navigation pane, which groups your Access objects. This is similar to the desktop database interface and can be filtered easily to help you locate a specific design object. This means that you can use design features from both the table in the Table Selector and the table contained in the navigation pane.

In the navigation pane, the views are listed under the heading Forms. This is because the terminology used in the navigation pane comes from desktop databases.

Show the navigation pane

1 Click the Settings/Actions charm in the Table Selector to see the available options.

2 Click Navigation Pane on the Home tab of the ribbon.

3 Use the Search box to filter the results.

4 Right-click a table to see options similar to those available from the Table Selector.

5 Click each view that is displayed for a specific table. These are the different views of the table that Access has automatically constructed.

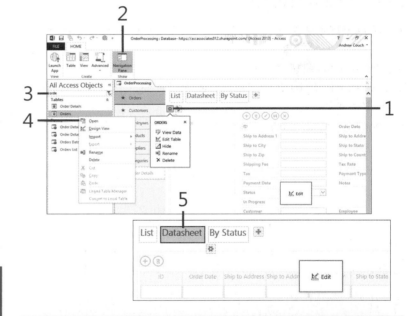

> ✓ **TIP** If you select the Open shortcut on the Table Selector menu or select View Data from the options on the Table Selector, you can type data directly into your tables without the need to display the views in a web browser.

> ⚠ **CAUTION** If you click Edit, you will not change the table design, but you will change the design of the selected view. We will look at the View Layout features in Section 3, "Modifying a Web App."

> ✓ **TIP** After Access has automatically created views of your data, if you add new fields to the table, the views automatically change to include your new fields—a very powerful feature. But if you edit the views, this capability is lost. This balances the needs of people who want Access to control the layouts with those users who want finer control of the layouts.

Adding a blank table

As an alternative to using a predefined table template for your Web App, you can create individual tables and then relate these tables by using lookups. Access allows you to either start with a completely empty Web App or add to an existing Web App you have created by using a template.

The first field in any table is created automatically; it is called ID. This is an AutoNumber field and cannot be removed because a Web App table needs a unique numeric field as a primary key.

When you add a new table (for example, *Countries*), Access automatically creates two views (for example, *Countries List* and *Countries Datasheet*).

Add a blank table

1 Click Table from the Home tab of the ribbon. Then select Add A New Blank Table.

2 Select an appropriate data type for each new field name.

3 Change any appropriate field properties. When you click any field name, the lower area of the screen displays the properties for the field.

4 Click Save to save the table.

5 Type a table name, and click OK.

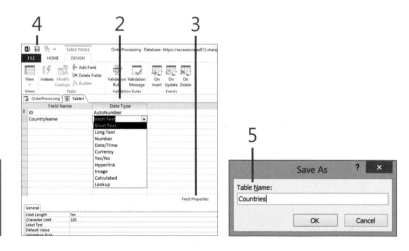

> ✓ **TIP** Although the ID field cannot be removed, you can rename this field. For example, in a Customer table, you could rename the field ID to CustomerID if you think that this would help when you are working with the database structure, such as when designing queries.

Launching a Web App

When you are creating your Web App, you can modify and adjust what is contained in the application, but it is not until you launch the app that you can enter data and explore how to interact with the app through your web browser.

When you view your data in a browser, you can see the action bar, which enables you to add, delete, and save changes to your data. An exception is in the Datasheet view, where changes are recorded when you click onto a new record. Otherwise, you need to use the action bar to save changes to the record you are editing.

Launch a Web App

1 Click Launch App from the Home tab of the ribbon.

2 Click a table in which you want to enter data.

3 Type data in some of the available fields.

4 On the action bar, click to save your changes.

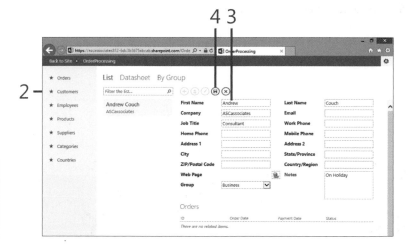

> **TIP** The action bar on a view can be customized to contain up to 10 icons. It is often a good idea to hide rather than delete icons that you do not want to show because, if deleted, these built-in icons cannot be easily added back to the action bar.

Working with the List view

The List view is the first of three presentations of data shown for the selected table. The List view is split into two areas. The first area, called the list control, shows a simple tabular list of the records on the left side of the page, from which you can select a specific record. The full details of that record are displayed in the second detail area, on the right side of the List view. As new records are added or removed, the list control area automatically updates when the changes in the detail area are saved.

Work with the List view

1 Click List.

2 Click the Edit button on the action bar.

3 Look for a field that displays the text Find. This is the new Autocomplete control. (In our example, both the Customer and Employee choices are Autocomplete controls.)

4 As you type into an Autocomplete control, any matches are displayed. The control also has an <Add A New Item> option. Click this option.

5 After choosing to add a new item, type new data values.

6 Click the Save button on the action bar.

7 Close the window; your newly created record is now displayed as having been selected in the Autocomplete control.

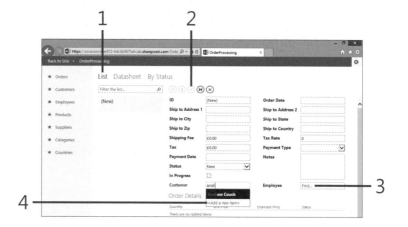

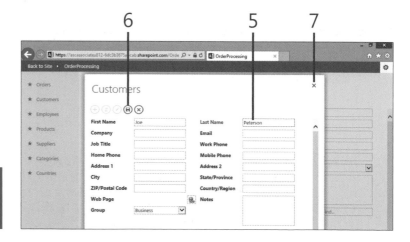

> ✓ **TIP** In our example for the Orders view, below the main order you can see an area for displaying and entering order details. This uses another new control, called the Related Items Control (RELIC).

Working with the Datasheet view

The Datasheet view is the second of three presentations for data; this presentation provides a tabulation of the data and can be scrolled left to right.

When working with the Datasheet view to enter new data, you can start by typing into a blank row or by clicking the plus sign (+) on the action bar. To edit an existing row, type into a cell in the row. Records and changes are saved when you click a cell in another row.

The columns can be reordered and adjusted in width, and the rows can be sorted and filtered.

Work with the Datasheet view

1 Click Datasheet.

2 Type new data in a record. After you move out of the first field, the record selector on the left changes to a pencil shape.

3 Click a cell in any other row to save your changes.

4 Point to a column heading until the mouse shape changes to a cross. Click, hold, and drag the column to a new column position to reorder the column.

5 Click the drop-down arrow to display options for filtering and sorting data.

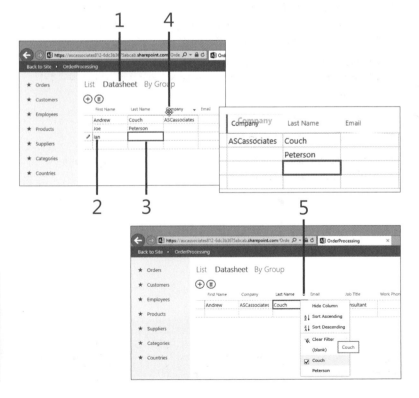

> **TIP** Although it might appear that you cannot filter by multiple choices, this is not the case. After making a selection and filtering the data (the value Couch in our example), when you redisplay the filtering options, a check box will appear against the current filter value. Making a second choice (Peterson) adds another filter value, and the data will then filter by both choices.

Working with a summary view

A summary view is the third way of presenting data. Summary views created by templates typically use By Group as the label in the view selector. Summary views allow you to view a tabulation of data by grouping on a particular field. You can also filter the grouping field to limit the displayed groups.

A summary view combines a list of values with the related item control, which tabulates the matched records. The view is read-only.

Work with a summary view

1 Find a suitable table that has a By Group view. Click By Group.

2 Type any filtering data to reduce the visible groups.

3 Click the search symbol, and then click a desired group to display the members of the group.

4 In views created by templates, you can click the tabulated record to display a popup window for a detailed record.

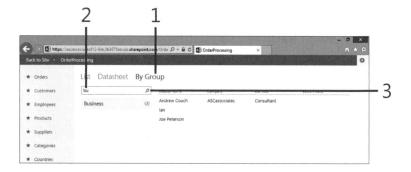

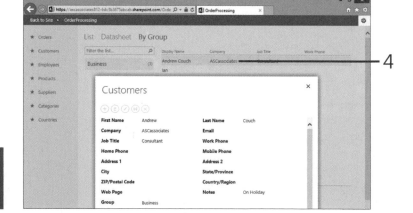

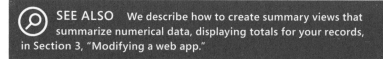

SEE ALSO   We describe how to create summary views that summarize numerical data, displaying totals for your records, in Section 3, "Modifying a web app."

Finding your site and navigating to the team site

Your team site contains all your Web Apps. If you start by launching your Web App, you can use the Navigate Up menu choice to get to the site, or you can get to the site from your main Office 365 Account area. On the left menu, the Recent choices will display a list of Recent items. Use the Site Contents to display all items on the site.

If you are using a different computer, where your copy of Access does not have your site located as a Recent item, you can go to Team Site – Site Contents and open your Web App in Access.

Find a site

1 Click Back To Site.

2 Click Site Contents.

3 Click the ellipse button (...) to display other options for an application.

4 Close the options for the application, and click a Web App to display the application in the browser window.

5 Click Customize In Access.

6 Click Open to launch your Web App in Access, and answer OK to any further security prompts to open the Web App on your desktop.

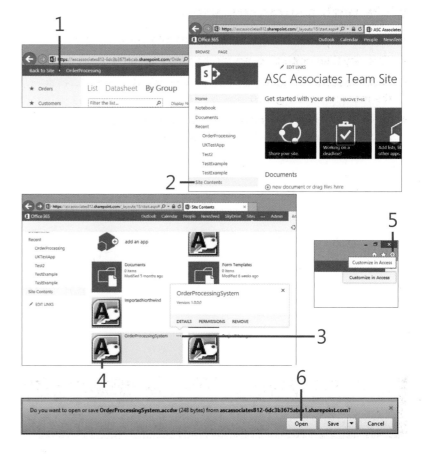

Creating a Web App using a template

Access has a number of application templates that you can use to create complete applications. When these templates start with a name beginning with *Desktop*, they generate desktop databases, and the other templates will generate Web Apps.

After you start Access, the initial screen shows a choice of both desktop and Web App database templates.

Create a Web App using a template

1 Click the appropriate template in the Office Start Screen.

2 Type a name for your Web App in the App Name text box.

3 Type your Office 365 URL in the Web Location text box, or select from the Available Locations list.

4 Click Create.

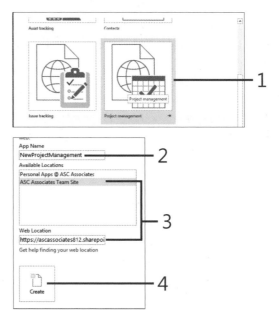

Modifying a Web App

3

In this section, we look at some of the common activities you might want to perform in modifying and adding to the standard features that are provided when you create a Web App.

While a desktop database draws a distinction between lookup fields and creating relationships, a Web App merges the concepts of lookups and relationships. Therefore, you will not find any part of the Web App that can display relationships because they have been built into the process of creating a lookup.

When you create a table in a Web App, you automatically get two great views created for you, Datasheet and List, which you can use by navigating to the appropriate table in the vertical Table Selector. Each table can have a number of views, and the views can also display data from other tables or queries in the App.

In this section:

- Importing from an Access desktop database
- Changing the design of a table
- Creating a lookup/relationship
- Designing with the List Details view, the Datasheet view, the summary view, and the blank view
- Open, rename, duplicate, or delete a view
- Creating a query
- Modifying the Table Selector
- Working with reports

Importing from an Access desktop database

If you have an existing Access Desktop database, you can import the tables and, optionally, the data from that database into a new Web App. The data can be imported from a variety of sources, including an Access desktop database.

Where possible, the process of importing data will also import relationships between your tables and convert these to look-ups. If you don't have an appropriate database available to investigate the techniques described in this section, you can refer to Section 1, "About this book," for information about how to download the sample data that we have used in preparing this section of the book.

We start with a new custom Web App into which we will import existing data.

Import an Access database

1 Click Table on the Home tab of the ribbon.

2 On the Add Tables screen, click Access.

3 Click Browse.

4 Locate the Access desktop database file. (If you do not already have an accessible database file, you will not be able to complete any further steps until you have installed or created one.)

5 Click Open.

6 Click OK.

(continued on next page)

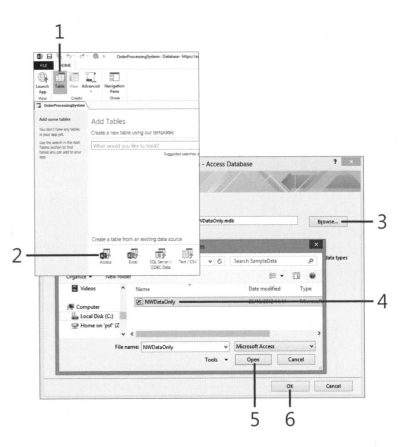

Import an Access database *(continued)*

7 Select the tables to import, or click Select All.

8 Click Options to display further options when importing data.

9 Choose to import or exclude the relationships.

10 Choose to import either definitions only or definitions and data.

11 Click OK. During the import process, your existing relationships will be converted into Lookup data types.

12 Right-click the table that has relationships to other tables, and select Edit Table.

The relationship is now shown as a Lookup data type.

13 Close the table.

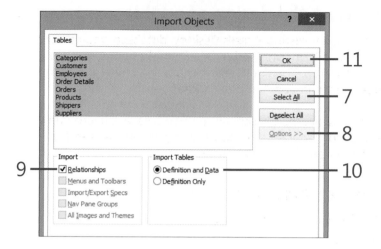

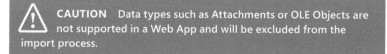

⚠ **CAUTION** Data types such as Attachments or OLE Objects are not supported in a Web App and will be excluded from the import process.

Changing the design of a table

In Section 2, "Creating a custom Web App," we demonstrate how the desktop interface can allow you to display content both by using the Table Selector and by showing the navigation pane. You can use either of these interfaces to enter design view and change the design of your table. Here we show how to enter design view from the table in the Table Selector. (If you prefer the navigation pane, right-click an object to see similar options.)

In Access 2013, the available data types for fields have changed, and the most obvious change is that a Text field is now called a Short Text field and a Memo field is called a Long Text field. However, there are some other differences between the available data types in a Web App compared to a desktop database.

Change the design of a table

1   Right-click a table, and select Edit Table.

2   Click the Data Type drop-down arrow to see the available choices of data types.

(continued on next page)

Change the design of a table *(continued)*

The following table describes the data types that are available. For each data type, we show in parentheses the SQL Server data type that is used to store the data.

Data type	Description (SQL Server data type)
Short Text	Unicode Text field allowing a maximum of 4,000 characters (nvarchar(4000)). The default is 220 characters.
Long Text	Large amounts of text (corresponds to a nvarchar(max), 2^30–1 bytes in SQL Server 2012).
Number	Whole number with no decimal places (int), Floating-point number (float), and Fixed-point number (decimal(28,6), six decimal places).
Date/Time	Date (date), Time (time(3)), and Date with Time (datetime2(3)).
Currency	Money (decimal(28,6)).
Yes/No	(bit) True, False (default is False).
Hyperlink	Large amount of text (nvarchar(max)).
Image	Binary Image data (varbinary(max) 2^31-1 bytes in SQL Server 2012).
Calculated	Calculated field using SQL Server functions. Storage depends on expression.
Lookup	Creates a foreign key lookup. (Lookup foreign key stored as integer (int)).

> ✓ **TIP** Behind the scenes in Office 365, your data is stored in Microsoft SQL Server for a corporate solution or using Microsoft SQL Azure in conjunction with Office 365. SQL Server is similar to Access in being a relational database but it is more scalable (so it can handle more data that the normal Access Database), and SQL Azure is a version of SQL Server that it is the platform that Microsoft use to deliver data on the web. We only explain the underlying SQL Server data types here for reference; you don't need to learn anything new to use this.

Creating a lookup/relationship

A Web App allows you to create a lookup, which ties or relates data between tables. (The relationship concept is described in Section 4, "Creating a desktop database," for a desktop database.) The Web App does not have a separate area for viewing relationships. You can view them for individual tables by selecting Modify Lookups in the Table Tools group on the Design tab.

A Web App simplifies the design process by keeping you focused on creating lookups between tables. The terms *relationship* and *lookup* mean the same thing in a Web App, and in the popup window used to create the lookup, you will see options similar to those available for creating relationships in a desktop database.

Create a lookup

1 On a blank line in the Field Name column, type a name for the lookup.

2 In the Data Type column, select the Lookup data type.

3 Select the option to look up data from a table or query.

4 Select the table from which you want to get a value.

5 Select the field to display.

6 Choose how the related records are managed.

7 Click OK.

(continued on next page)

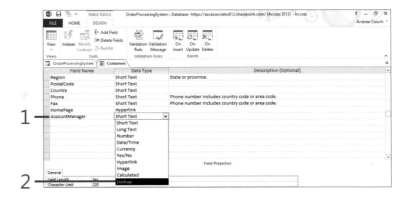

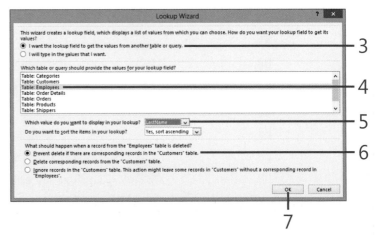

 TIP The lower part of the Lookup Wizard screen displays the optional rules for defining a relationship between the tables.

Create a lookup *(continued)*

8 Click Save.

9 Click View.

10 When viewing the data, you can see the Autocomplete control displaying the lookup data.

11 In the browser, you can type data into the new field that was automatically added to the List Details view.

8

10

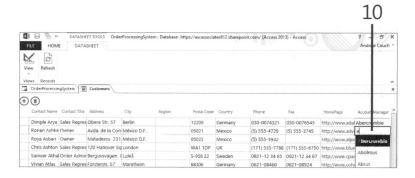

11

> **TIP** If you have not changed the design of any views associated with your table, the added field automatically displays in the updated List Details view and Datasheet view for the table.

Designing with a List Details view

A view in a Web App is similar to a form in a desktop database. There are four types of views; List Details, Datasheet, Summary, and Blank. The List Details view is a powerful feature. In its simplest form, it has a vertical tabulation of the available records on the left side of the view, and when a record is selected, the record details are displayed on the right side of the view.

The layout capabilities of this view mean that as you delete, add, or move fields, the layout automatically moves other fields to accommodate the position of the new fields, simplifying the process of altering the view. The Record Source field (where the view gets the data) allows you to choose from the table or any queries that include the table.

Create a List Details view

1 Locate the object in the Table Selector.

2 Click the plus sign.

3 Type a name for the view, select List Details as the view type, and select the record source.

4 Click Add New View.

5 When the new view is displayed, click Edit.

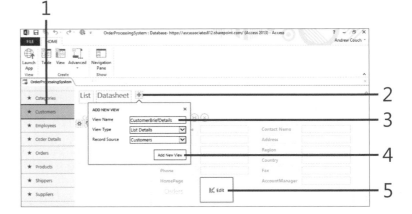

✓ **TIP** In the lower part of a view, you may have a related item control (Orders in our example). To resize the control, click to select it (it will change color when selected); you can then grab the top edge of the control (the mouse shape will change when hovering over the edge) and resize the control.

Remove fields

1 Click a field.

2 Hold down the Ctrl key to select multiple fields and labels. Press the Delete key to remove the fields.

3 Select any other fields to be repositioned, and drag the fields to close up white space.

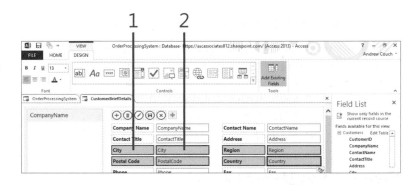

TIP By using the Ctrl key, you can select multiple controls and move them around the layout. After selecting the controls, move the mouse over the area until a crossing arrows symbol is displayed, and then click the left mouse button and drag the controls to a new position. As you move the controls around, other controls will change position, opening up a gap into which you can position the new controls.

Add fields

1 Select a field from the Field List on the right side.

2 Drag the field to a new position on the display area.

3 As you move over other fields, they will make space to allow the new control to be positioned.

CAUTION Although you can select multiple fields in the Field List, when you use the dragging action to add the fields, only the first field will be added.

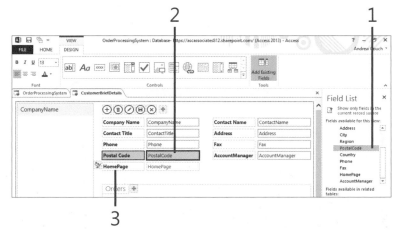

Designing with a Datasheet view

A Datasheet view is the simplest view to create. This view tabulates the data and displays your fields as columns. Although it is extremely simple, when combined with the abilities to filter data, sort data, and reorder the columns, it is a very powerful method to quickly present a tabulation of your data.

In a List Details view, before you can edit data, you need to use the action bar to put the record into edit mode. However, in the Datasheet view, you can edit data without doing this and move to the next record to continue editing another record, which automatically saves the changes from the previously edited row. This is a unique and very powerful feature of a Web App datasheet.

The Record Source property (where the view gets the data) allows you to choose from the table or any queries that include the table.

Create a Datasheet view

1 Locate the table in the Table Selector.

2 Click the plus sign.

3 Type a name for the view, select Datasheet as the view type, and select the record source.

4 Click Add New View.

5 When the new view is displayed, click Edit.

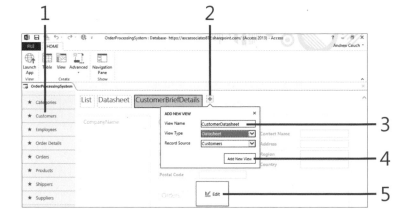

Format a field

1 Click a field to format.

2 Click the formatting charm.

3 Change the formatting.

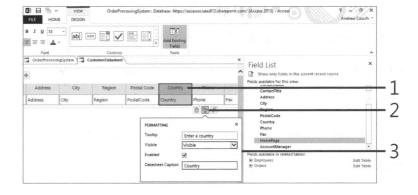

Designing with a summary view

A summary view allows you to summarize data by calculating a sum or average. You need to choose a table or query with numerical fields before you can work with many of the best features in this type of view.

The Record Source field (where the view gets the data) allows you to choose from the table or any queries that include the table.

If you have been creating tables by using templates, you might already have seen examples of a summary view, which would appear as a third available view on some of the tables. When you create your own tables, a Web App will automatically create a List view and a Datasheet view.

Create a summary view

1 Locate the object in the Table Selector.

2 Click the plus sign.

3 Type a name for the view, select Summary as the view type, and select the record source.

4 Click Add New View.

5 When the new view is displayed, click Edit.

(continued on next page)

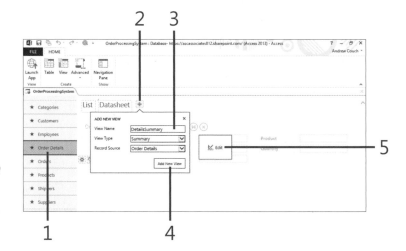

Create a summary view *(continued)*

6 Click the control list shown on the left.

7 Click the Data charm next to the list control.

8 In the Data popup window, choose the field to group by, type a header for the calculation, and choose the field and calculation type.

9 Close the Data popup window.

10 Click the details area on the right.

11 Click the Data charm next to the details area.

12 Define the fields to summarize.

13 When displaying a summary view in a browser, click each record in the control list on the left to see the summary details on the right change to match the selected record.

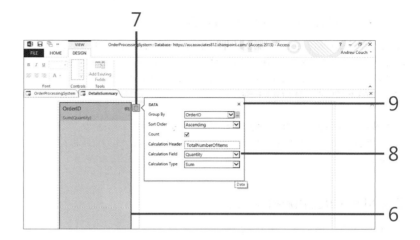

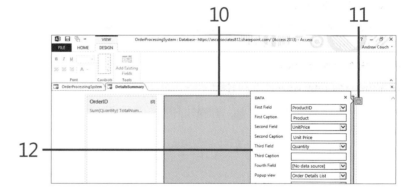

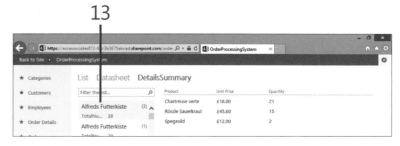

Designing with a blank view

A blank view will create a presentation that does not display any fields from the table. This can give you a greater amount of control over what data is displayed, although it might involve more work in creating the view.

Normally, a view displays information from the table associated with the selected table and related tables, but you can add a view that displays information from an unrelated table. In this

example, we will add to the Products table View Selector a view that allows you to browse through the Category records but not display any associated record from the Products table.

Create a blank view

1 Locate the object in the Table Selector.

2 Click the plus sign.

3 Type a name for the view, select Blank as the view type, and then select the record source.

4 Click Add New View.

5 When the new view is displayed, click Edit.

6 Click the Data icon.

7 Change the record source.

8 Close the Data popup window.

(continued on next page)

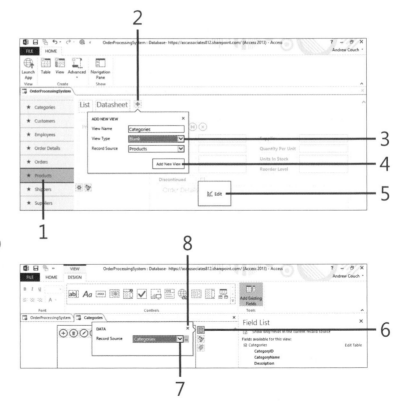

Create a blank view *(continued)*

9 In the Field List, select a field.

10 Drag the field onto the blank view.

11 After you have saved the changes, the View Selector for the table has a view that displays information from another table without involving the table associated with the selected table name caption in the View Selector.

10   9

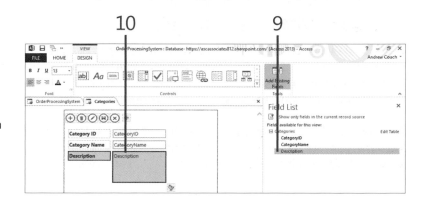

11

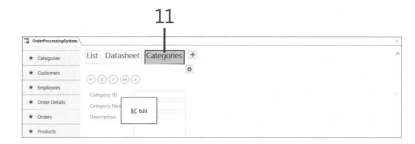

Open, rename, duplicate, or delete a view

When you display a view in Access, you can use the Settings/ Actions charm next to the view name to perform basic operations on the view. The options are Open In Browser, Edit, Rename, Duplicate, and Delete.

When you choose Open In Browser, the view immediately displays in the browser window, saving you from having to locate

the table and then select the view. The Rename option allows you to change the name of the view, the Duplicate option makes a copy of a view, and the Delete option removes the view.

This task will demonstrate how, when editing a view, you can switch to the table design and modify the structure of the table.

Change a table design when editing a view

1 Click the Settings/Actions charm.

2 Select Edit.

3 If you are editing a view and displaying the Field List, you will see a link to edit the design of the table. Click the Edit Table option to change the design of the table.

(continued on next page)

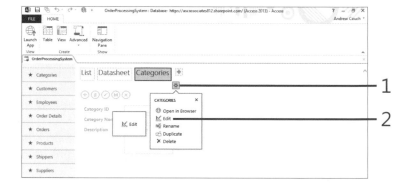

> ✓ **TIP** If you switch to design view on the table, you will find that you need to close any open views before you can save any changes that you make to the table.

Change a table design when
editing a view *(continued)*

4 Add a new field name.

5 Click Save. (You will not be able to save changes until you close any open views that refer to this table.)

6 Click the tab with the open view.

7 Close the view. If you now repeat step 5, you can save the changes to the design of the table.

5

4

6   7

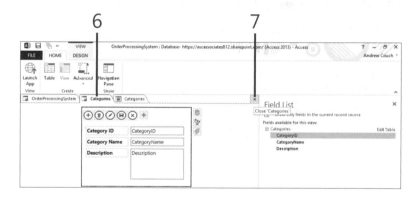

Creating a query

A query provides a powerful mechanism for filtering and sorting data. It can also be used to bring together data from several tables or other queries in a single presentation.

Like a table, a query can be opened to display data in the design interface without showing the results in the browser. To display the results in the browser, you need to create a view that uses the query.

In Section 7, "Modifying data using queries," we describe how you can create action queries that modify data in a desktop database—for example, updating a set of rows. These action queries are not available in a Web App.

Create a query

1 Click Advanced on the Home tab of the ribbon.

2 Select Query.

3 From the Show Table Dialog box, select one or more queries or tables from the Show Table dialog box by double-clicking each table.

4 Click Close when you have finished making selections.

(continued on next page)

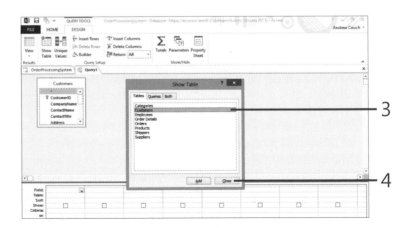

Create a query *(continued)*

5 Add the fields from the source data into the query grid by double-clicking each field listed in the table.

6 Click Save.

7 Type a name for the query, and click OK to save it.

8 Click View.

9 Select Datasheet View to test the query.

6

5

7

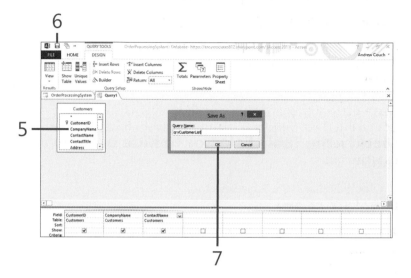

8

9

SEE ALSO For a detailed explanation of how to construct select queries, see Section 6, "Selecting data using queries."

Modifying the Table Selector

In a Web App, you interact with the data by selecting a table from the Table Selector and then selecting an available view associated with the table from a list of available views, called the View Selector.

Each table in the Table Selector can be modified to rename captions or hide a table caption without affecting the underlying table. This means that the Table Selector works like a main menu for the application, and the View Selector works like a submenu.

Modify the Table Selector to hide or show a table

1 Click the table in the Table Selector.

2 Click the Settings/Actions charm.

3 Select Hide.

4 The table name caption in the Table Selector is now grayed out.

> **⚠ CAUTION** If an item is deleted, the underlying table will also be deleted.

> **✓ TIP** After you hide a table, the table name caption will be grayed out and moved to the bottom of the Table Selector. The table name caption will be hidden when you are viewing results in a browser.

Change a table icon

1 Click the formatting charm.

2 Choose an icon for the Table Selector item.

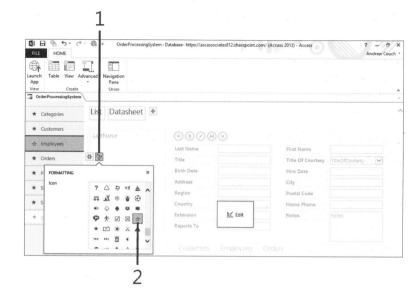

Working with reports

Although a Web App does not have a reporting feature that can be displayed in a browser window, you can create reports as described in Section 10, "Preparing data to print using reports," in a desktop database that is linked to the data held in the Web App.

The first step is to use the Info option on the File menu to create a desktop database that is connected to your data.

Create a report database

1   On the File menu, select the Info option and then click Create Reports.

2   Choose a location, and provide a name for the reporting database.

3   Click Save.

4   The new reporting database opens, and on the left, you can see a list of the tables that are linked to your Web App. Double-click a table in the navigation pane to display the data.

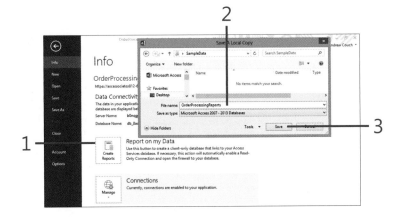

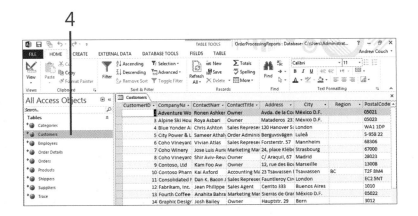

Creating a desktop database

4

A desktop database uses tables to hold your data and is stored on your local computer or network. The data is displayed in rows (horizontal layout), with each row including a list of column or field names (vertical layout) like a worksheet. Using database tables differs from using several worksheets in a workbook. Generally, you will find it more natural and beneficial to create additional tables than to create more worksheets. Also, the rules for data consistency in any column are more strictly enforced in a database, which helps you to improve the quality of the data that you are recording.

Each field in the table can be of a different data type, depending on the data to be held. Storing data in the correct field type is important because you can take advantage of special features in the database—for example, displaying a date picker when working with date data, or validating that sensible data is being entered for the chosen field type, or relating the data in one table to a list of values in another table.

A database normally consists of more than one table, and having the tables correctly related to one another will save you a lot of subsequent work. An invaluable tool in Access is the Lookup Wizard, which can automatically build the required relationships between the tables.

In this section:

- Creating a blank desktop database
- Creating a table in design and layout views
- Working with data parts in layout view
- Creating a table by using application parts
- Adding a primary key
- Improving performance by indexing data
- Validating data in a field
- Formatting a field
- Recording changes to text and rich text formatting
- Creating relationships by using the Lookup Wizard
- Viewing and adding relationships

Creating a blank desktop database

After starting Access as described at the beginning of Section 2, "Creating a custom Web App," you can use one of the available template databases, or you can create a blank database as described in this section.

Access offers you the flexibility to use templates of commonly encountered database structures or to start with an empty database into which you can either import existing data or create a solution tailored to your specific needs.

Create a blank desktop database

1 Click Blank Desktop Database.

2 Type a name for your database.

3 Select a file location in which to save the database.

4 Click Create.

5 When the new blank database opens in layout view (described later in this section), you will see that Access has created a table called Table1. At this point, we can close this table without saving any changes to the new table. Click the Close button to close the table.

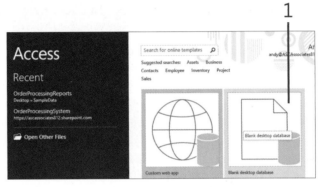

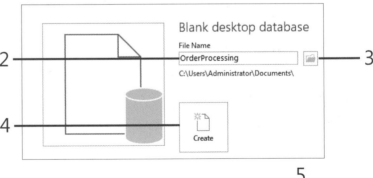

> **TIP** The templates for a desktop application all begin with the word *desktop*, and you can scroll down the list of templates to see these. Other templates are for creating a Web App.

The following table lists the available data types when you are adding fields to a table in a desktop database.

Data type	Description
Short Text	Text up to 255 characters. In earlier versions of Access, this data type was called Text.
Long Text	Large amounts of text, up to 65,536 characters. In earlier versions of Access, this data type was called Memo.
Number	Field Size property provides for Byte, Integer, Long Integer (default), Single, Double, Replication ID, Decimal.
Date/Time	Date and Time field.
Currency	Currency field.
AutoNumber	Sequential Automatic Number, Long Integer (default).
Yes/No	True/False (default is False).
OLE Object	Can hold images or other documents.
Hyperlink	Hyperlink to the Internet and local documents.
Attachment	Allows multiple documents to be saved.
Calculated	Calculated field.
Lookup	Creates a foreign key lookup.

Creating a table in design view

Creating tables in design view gives you the greatest control over how the fields and properties are set, but it also involves more work than other techniques. Each field in the table design has a set of properties that you can safely leave at the default values. You can change these properties as you gain a deeper understanding of the product's features.

A fantastic feature of Access is that the design view can always be used to modify an existing table structure, regardless of which technique you use to create the table.

Create a table

1 Click the Create tab.

2 Click Table Design.

3 Type a name in the Field Name column for each field you want—for example, **CustomerName**.

4 In the Data Type drop-down list, select a data type for each field—for example, Short Text. (At the end of this exercise, a table describes the data types that are available.)

5 Click Save.

6 Provide a name for the table, and click OK.

(continued on next page)

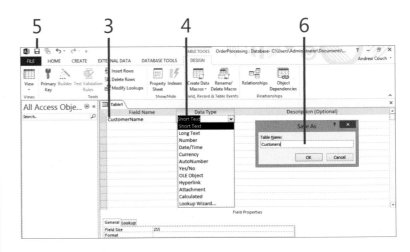

> **TIP** Designers sometimes begin table names with a prefix, such as *tbl*—for example, *tblCustomers*—to distinguish tables from queries (which are prefixed with qry) when both appear in one list. Having a naming convention is a good idea when you're creating complex databases.

Create a table *(continued)*

7 If you have not created a primary key, you will be prompted to add a key. Click Yes to add a primary key.

8 After saving your table, the new ID primary key is added to the table.

9 The table now appears in the navigation pane.

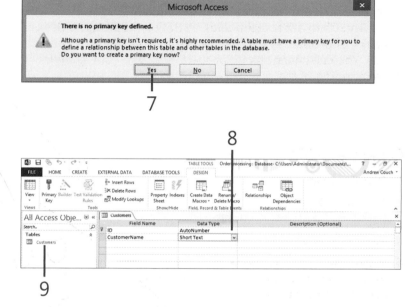

✔ **TIP** Because there are several different choices here for numbers, you might find it easiest to use a Long Integer for whole numbers and use a Double for numbers with decimal places.

✔ **TIP** If you know which field(s) would make a good choice for a unique primary key, select the fields and click the primary key button. A primary key must be unique for each record in the table and cannot be null (blank). You can use more than one field to create a composite primary key, where each field doesn't contain unique values, but the *combination* of fields will always be unique.

Creating a table in layout view

The layout view in Access can be used for tables, forms, and reports, and it enables you to make design changes without using the more complex design view. You can make changes and, at the same time, see how the design will finally look. In layout view, you have less control over detailed choices, but you have a faster and more intuitive interface through which to interact with the table.

In layout view, Access automatically adds a unique AutoNumber primary key, called *ID*, to your blank table design. After working in the layout view, you can always switch to the design view to refine your choices.

Create a table

1 Click the Create tab.

2 Click Table.

3 Click the Click To Add drop-down list.

4 Select a data type.

5 Replace the default caption Field1 with a name for the field.

6 Click Save.

7 Provide a name for the table, and click OK.

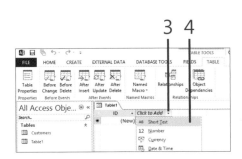

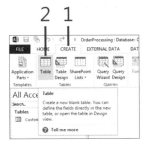

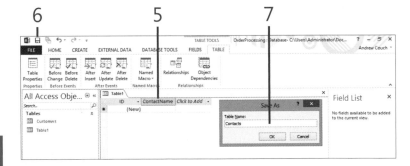

> ✓ **TIP** At this point, you will find it easier both to close the Field List pane on the right and to switch from the Table Tools tab to the Fields tab, which displays the full set of choices for setting properties on each field.

Change field captions and descriptions

1 Click the Fields tab.

2 Click the ContactName field.

3 Click Name & Caption.

4 In the Enter Field Properties popup window, change the Caption field to Contact Name, and for the Description type **Name of company contact**.

5 Click OK. The title for the column is now displayed with a space via the Caption property, and the description will be displayed on the lower left on the status bar.

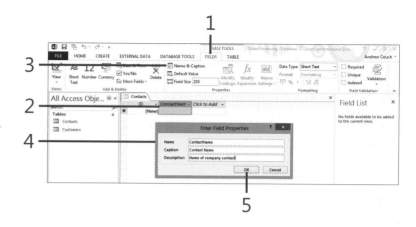

TIP   One of the most common field data types to add is Short Text. The default field size is 255 characters (shown on the ribbon below Default Value). If you need only 20 characters, reducing the field size can help prevent you from accidentally storing more information than can be displayed—for example, when you have positioned a field on a form or report to be a specific size. Otherwise, do not worry about making it smaller just to save space.

Working with data parts in layout view

Data parts, which are shown in layout view in the More Fields drop-down list, allow you to quickly add one or more fields to a table from a list of prepared fields. For example, adding an Address will add the fields Address, City, StateProvince, ZipPost, and CountryRegion to your table.

You can also select any number of existing fields that you have added to a table, and add them to this list of data parts so that you can easily add those fields to another table.

Add a data part

1   With a table open in layout view (for the Customers table in our example), click the Click To Add box at the right of the datasheet. The cursor will then be positioned to add the new fields at the end of the datasheet.

2   Click the Fields tab.

3   Click More Fields.

4   Scroll down the list of available fields, and click the Address field.

5   The new fields are automatically added to the design of the table.

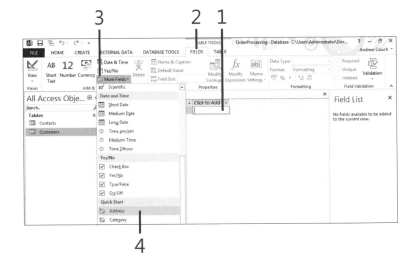

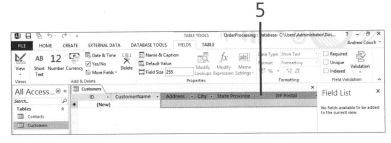

Create a new data part

1 With the table in layout view, click the titles of one or more fields. (If necessary, you can use the Shift key to select multiple fields that are next to each other.)

2 Click the Fields tab.

3 Click More Fields.

4 Scroll to the bottom of the list, and select Save Selection As New Data Type.

5 Type a name for the data type.

6 Type a description for the data type.

7 Select a category in which to display the data type.

8 Click OK.

9 In the message that appears, noting where your new data type has been saved in the file system, click OK.

10 If you click More Fields again, you can see that your new data type has been added to the list of available data types. You can now add this new data type to a different table by following the steps described in the preceding exercise, "Add a data part," on page 50.

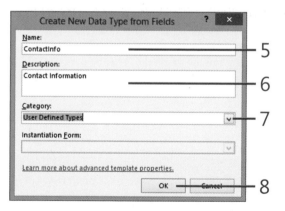

Creating a table by using application parts

Application parts are predefined templates for creating popular layouts by using different Access objects. Depending on the part you select, you could have a series of steps that further integrate the chosen part with your application. These parts can enable you to add a great new feature to your database with minimum effort, although the choices for tables here are quite limited.

Choosing an application part can add several objects into your database, including supporting forms and reports.

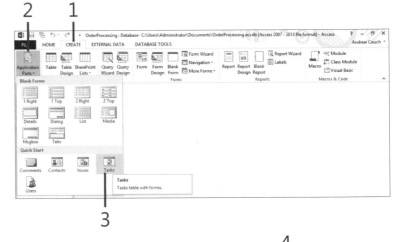

Add an application part

1 Click the Create tab.

2 Click Application Parts.

3 Select an application part.

4 In the Create Relationship popup window, select the table to relate this part to, if one is available, and click Next.

(continued on next page)

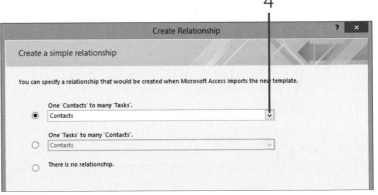

> ⚠️ **CAUTION** If you decide to use a primary key, such as an ID, rather than, for example, the contact name, you will need to later use the table design view to adjust your lookup field width because the drop-down lookup box has 0 width when it is a numeric key field.

Add an application part *(continued)*

5 Choose the field to look up.

6 Type a name for the lookup column.

7 Click Create.

8 Three new design objects have been added to the database.

9 The new lookup field now displays data from our existing Contacts table.

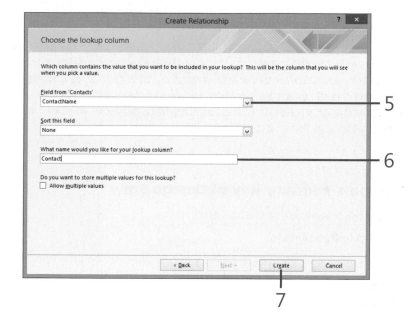

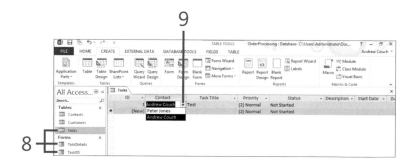

TIP Access supports lookups that can store multiple values. This feature saves you from creating additional tables, which would otherwise be required to hold the multiple selections. In the example, we could have made this selection store multiple contacts against a single task.

TIP It is also possible to create your own application part to allow you to quickly add a set of objects to your database. The following article from the Access Team provides details on how to do this: *blogs.office.com/b/microsoft-access/archive/2010/03/31/access-2010-application-parts-and-quick-start-fields.aspx.*

Adding a primary key

It is recommended that every table has a primary key. This key enables you to create relationships between tables of data. If you can't easily decide on a key, when you first save a new table Access will warn you that there is no primary key and will then add one if you agree to having an automatic number for the primary key.

The primary key needs to be unique for every row in the table, and it can consist of one or multiple fields. The primary key must be given a value before the record can be saved, which is another reason why AutoNumber data types (an automatic sequence of numbers) are a popular choice for the primary key. The primary key can be added or changed in both design and layout views.

Define a primary key in design view

1 Right-click the table in the navigation pane.

2 Select Design View.

3 Select one or more fields. (Use the Ctrl key, and click the field selector to pick multiple fields.)

4 Click Primary Key.

5 Click Save.

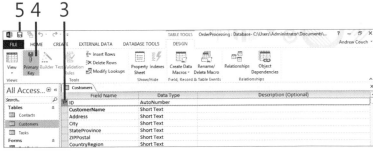

> ⚠️ **CAUTION** To be part of a primary key, each field forming part of the key must be given a value and must not contain NULL (no values). The combination of these fields must also be unique.

> ✓ **TIP** Web Apps support only numeric primary keys (normally AutoNumber data types), so this is a good choice if you later want to move your application to a Web App.

Improving performance by indexing data

If you went to a bookshop to find a book and started searching the bookshelves as you walked in, beginning with the first shelf, it would take a long time to find the book you wanted. Books in a shop are grouped together, often by topic, to make this task easier. This is the idea behind an index—you can find the book quicker by looking only at the shelves in a specific group. Indexes speed up data retrieval.

Access will automatically add indexes to your foreign key fields when you create relationships. You can add other indexes manually to improve the speed of retrieving data, but this also introduces a slight overhead when updating data. This is because editing the data can change the indexed value (which Access needs to maintain). Indexes work best on fields containing many different values.

Create an index

1 In the table design view, locate the field name you want to index.

2 In the Field Properties section, select an Index allowing duplicates.

3 You can display and manage all indexes in a table by using the Indexes popup window.

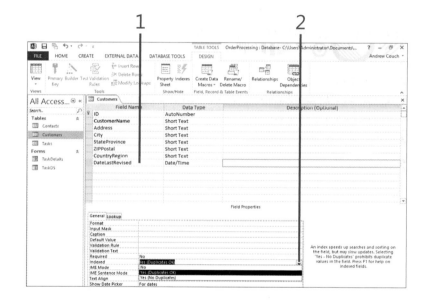

> **TIP** Don't bother indexing tables with less than several thousand entries. Don't index fields that have few distinct values—for example, a Yes/No field. Don't index foreign keys; Access will do that for you. Indexes are best added when a query or report is slow, and after adding the index, you can check to verify that the query is faster as a result of having added the index.

Validate that data in a field is of the correct type

You can validate the data entered into a field in the following ways:

- Choose the correct data type for the field. (If you choose a Date field, you can enter only valid dates.)

- Make a field required (you must enter a value for the field).

- Use an Input Mask to ensure that information, such as a telephone number, is entered in the correct pattern of digits.

- Add a validation rule, which allows more complex logic to

check that the values are correctly entered. There is also an option to add a default value for a field, which can help with validation.

- Make the choices for the field by selecting from a list of values, either by using a specific (hard-coded) set of values or by looking up the values from another table.

You can combine these techniques to provide the required level of data validation.

Make a field required and add an input mask

1 Set the Required option to Yes to force the entry of a value.

2 Click the Input Mask build button to open the Input Mask Wizard.

3 Choose an appropriate input mask.

4 Click Next.

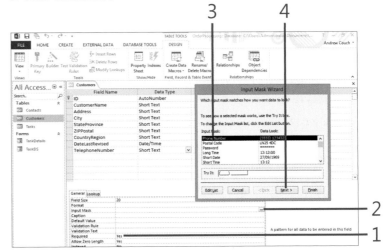

(continued on next page)

✓ **TIP** Allow Zero Length means that when you have a required text field, a user can type "" (empty string), which will be considered sufficient as a required value. If you do not want to allow this, set Allow Zero Length to No. Unless the field is required, you are unlikely to want to set this option to No.

Make a field required and add an input mask *(continued)*

5 Alter the pattern used in the mask if required. (At the end of this exercise, we have provided details of the mask symbols and their meaning.)

6 Change the placeholder character if you want a different symbol.

7 Click Next.

8 Select whether any symbols in the mask are stored with the data.

9 Click Finish.

10 This mask is now displayed in design view for the selected field.

The Input Mask consists of four sections, each separated by a semicolon (;).

- The first part contains the mask. See the upcoming table for a description of what can be entered in the mask.

- In the second part, 0 means store any literal characters, and 1 or blank means do not store literal characters.

- The third part specifies the character to be displayed in each position when you type into the mask. To use a space, enclose it in double quotes (" ").

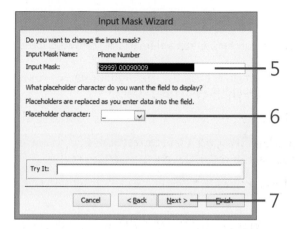

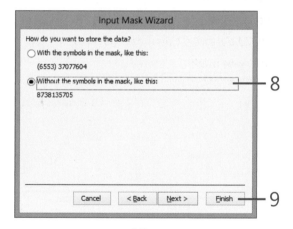

Add a field validation rule and default

1 Type a value or expression for Default Value. (Date() is today's date.)

2 Type a rule to check that the data is valid.

3 Add a text message to help the user when invalid data is entered, and save your design.

> ✓ **TIP** The validation rule also includes a build button (...), which can provide additional assistance in creating more complex expressions.

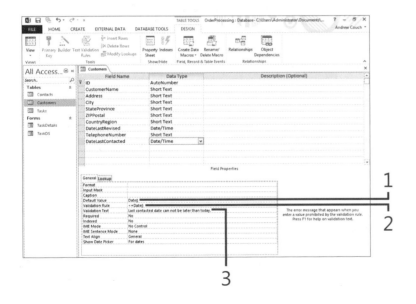

Character	Description (examples are for first part of the mask)
0	Digit (0 to 9, entry required, plus [+] and minus [–] signs not allowed). Example: 000 enters a number 987; 98 would not be allowed.
9	Digit or space (entry not required, plus and minus signs not allowed). Example: 999 would allow both 987 and 98 to be entered.
#	Digit or space (entry not required; spaces are displayed as blanks in Edit mode, but blanks are removed when data is saved; plus and minus signs allowed).
L	Letter (A to Z, entry required). Example: LLLL would allow the code DUCK but not DOG.
?	Letter (A to Z, entry optional). Example: ???? would allow both DOG and DUCK.
A	Letter or digit (entry required). Example: AAA would allow the code 99A but not 99.
a	Letter or digit (entry optional). Example: aaa would allow both 99A and 99.
&	Any character or a space (entry required). Example: 00&00 would allow 53/22 but not 53/2.
C	Any character or a space (entry optional). Example: 00C would allow 99B but not 9B.
<	Causes all characters to be converted to lowercase. Example: <LLLL would save Duck as duck.
>	Causes all characters to be converted to uppercase. Example: >LLLL would save duck as DUCK.

Character	Description (examples are for first part of the mask)
!	Causes the input mask to display from right to left, rather than from left to right. Characters typed into the mask always fill it from left to right. You can include the exclamation point anywhere in the input mask.
\	Causes the character that follows to be displayed as the literal character. For example, \(00\) would show 99 as (99).
" "	Characters enclosed in double quotation marks will be displayed literally. For example, "CODE-"999, would display 435 as CODE-435.

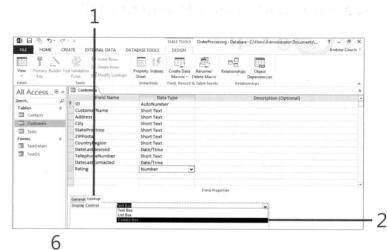

Create a lookup based on values

1 Click the Lookup tab in the Field Properties section.

2 Choose either Combo Box or List Box for displaying the value options.

3 Choose Value List as Row Source Type.

4 Click the build button for the Row Source.

5 Type the values as a list of choices, with an optional default, and then click OK.

6 Save your design.

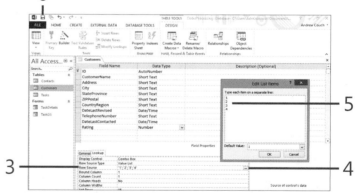

> **TIP** When you define lookups on a field and also use many of the other validation techniques described here, and then create a form, the form inherits copies of the defaults and field properties that you have defined on the field. If these values are likely to change, you might prefer to place the values in a table and look up the values from the table. Taking time to get these features defined in the table will save time when you start creating forms.

Comparing field values by using table validation

Each table is allowed one table validation rule; this rule can involve a number of comparisons between different combinations of fields.

If your table contains data, you will be offered the option of validating the existing data. If doing this, first copy your rule to the clipboard, because if the validation fails and you cancel the operation, the rule will be cleared and you will lose your work in building the rule.

Create a validation rule

1 In table design view, click Property Sheet.

2 Click the Validation Rule build button.

3 Double-click to select fields to construct your expression.

4 Type into the expression to complete the comparison, and click OK.

5 The validation rule is saved in the table properties.

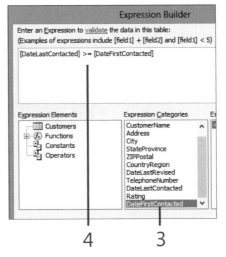

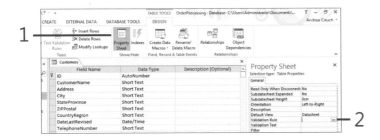

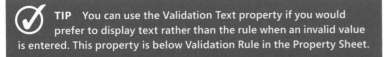

> **TIP** You can use the Validation Text property if you would prefer to display text rather than the rule when an invalid value is entered. This property is below Validation Rule in the Property Sheet.

Formatting a field

In addition to having an Input Mask property that controls how data is entered, a field also has a Format property that controls how data is displayed. Access will pick up your international settings for date/time and currency, and as long as you use one of the built-in formats, the data will be displayed in an appropriate regional format.

Format a field

1 Select the field.

2 On the General tab of the Field Properties section, select from an available format. (The formats shown here are for dates on a system set with UK international settings.)

The following table provides information for entering a custom format string.

Symbol	Description
(space)	Display spaces as literal characters.
"ABC"	Display anything inside quotation marks as literal characters.
!	Force left alignment instead of right alignment.
*	Fill available space with the next character.
\	Display the next character as a literal character. You can also display literal characters by placing quotation marks around them.
[color]	Display the formatted data in the color specified between the brackets. Available colors: Black, Blue, Green, Cyan, Red, Magenta, Yellow, White.

In addition to supporting a list of built-in formats, you can also use a combination of characters to specify a custom format for the data. The Format property can also include patterns with numerical data to display the data in specific colors, depending on the data value.

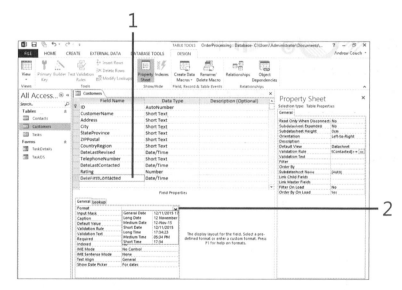

TIP We have listed here only a few of the basic formatting characters, and we refer you to the online help for a list of several tables of choices. In particular, there is an extensive range of date/time formats, and for numerical values, the format can have up to four parts (similar to an input mask), each of which can be associated with a different color, depending on whether the value is less than zero, zero, greater than zero, or null. For example, it could look like the following: $#,##0.00[Green];($#,##0.00)[Red];"Zero";"Null".

Recording changes to text and rich text formatting

The Long Text data type (which used to be called a Memo data type) has two very special features when it comes to formatting or recording text. The first is the field property in the table design view, which is called Append Only. When this is set, the field tracks all the text notes you add and allows you only to add notes, and not to change existing notes. The second property is support for formatted text, allowing you to change fonts, such as bold and italics, in your text.

Append Only and Rich Text for Long Text data

1 Select or add a Long Text field.

2 Change the Append Only field property to Yes.

3 Change the Text Format field property to Rich Text. (You might be asked to confirm this change, depending on whether your table contains data. Click Yes to confirm any prompt.)

4 Save your table.

5 Display your table in Datasheet view.

(continued on next page)

Append Only and Rich Text for Long Text data *(continued)*

6 Type a note.

7 You can also use the formatting options to change the fonts and color of the text, which is now held in an HTML format.

8 Click the next record to save your changes.

9 Edit the text in the note, and repeat steps 6 and 7 to make a couple of changes. The note appears to be allowing you to remove or change the existing text.

10 Right-click the Notes field, and select Show Column History.

11 The field history is displayed in a popup window for the Append Only Memo.

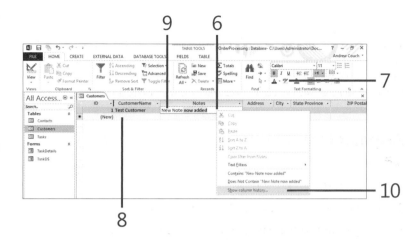

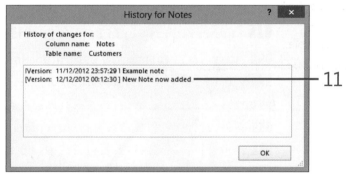

Creating relationships by using the Lookup Wizard

The Lookup Wizard is one of the most powerful features in Access, assisting you to relate data in one table that needs to look up data from another table.

The Lookup Wizard will also create a relationship between your main table and the lookup table and provides options to "Enforce Referential Integrity," which means preventing users from typing values that are not in the lookup table or from deleting values in the lookup table that have been used in the main table.

Create a lookup

1   In the table design view, move to a blank line in the Data Type column and select the Lookup Wizard in the drop-down list.

2   Select the option to look up values from another table or query.

3   Select the table from which you will look up a value, and click Next.

(continued on next page)

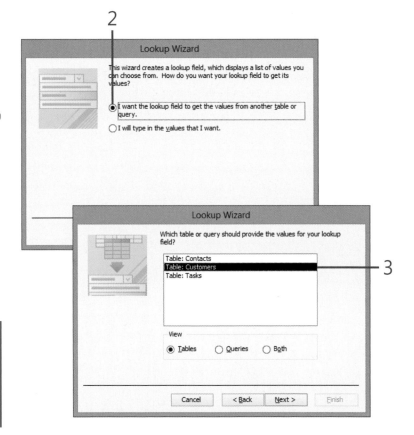

> **TIP**   Lookup fields allow you to look up data from a table or query or from a set of values that you type. Choosing to type a set of values works best when you have a set of choices that will not change over time. If you use a query, you cannot tie the tables together with a relationship. Performing lookups from a table is often the most flexible choice to make.

Create a lookup   (continued)

4 Select both the field value to save in the new field (ID) and the field value to display in the list (CustomerName). Click Next, on the following screen select any fields for sorting and click Next.

5 Choose whether to show or hide the key column. (Normally, if you have two columns selected, you would hide the primary key column.) Click Next.

6 Type a name for the lookup field.

7 Select the Enable Data Integrity check box to make sure that the list of customers and contacts that refer to the customers is always consistent.

8 Choose the Restrict Delete option to prevent customers from being deleted when they are referenced by a contact.

9 Click Finish.

10 Click Yes to save your changes.

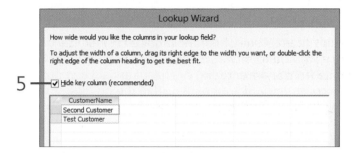

5

6

7

8

9

4

10

> ⚠️ **CAUTION** Choosing Cascade Delete on a relationship can be quite dangerous. In our example, it could mean that if you delete a customer, it would delete any contacts for that customer (depending on other relationship rules). In other circumstances, it could have a more dramatic impact on the data, so use the Cascade Delete option with great care!

Viewing relationships

Relationships sit at the very heart of what distinguishes a database from a worksheet; a relationship is a rule that cannot be subverted when you are entering or changing data and guarantees the consistency of your data (within the bounds of the rules). The relationship diagram can be a very misleading tool to work with in any database because it serves two purposes.

First, it is a roadmap you can delete tables and queries from the

diagram without changing anything. It is a passive picture that helps you see how tables are related to each other.

The second role of the diagram is exactly the opposite of the first use. When it comes to the actual relationships between tables (the lines joining them), the diagram is an active tool that allows you to create and delete rules (relationships) between your tables.

View relationships

1 Click the Database Tools tab.

2 Click Relationships.

3 Double-click a relationship line to display and/or change the relationship.

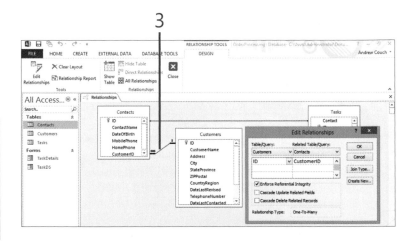

> **TIP** If you have a lot of tables on the relationship diagram, you can hide them all from the diagram and add just one table of interest to the diagram. Then, selecting that table and clicking Direct Relationships (in the Design tab of the ribbon) will display only those relationships between the selected table and other tables in the database. This is a very useful feature when you have a complex database with a large number of tables.

Deleting relationships

When we delete a relationship, we remove something from the database, but if you delete a table from the diagram, you are changing only the relationship picture. The table is not deleted from the database, and it can easily be added back to the diagram. When you save the relationship diagram, you are saving only a picture. It is when you delete or create relationships that the database gets changed.

Delete a relationship

1 Click the relationship line, which will become thicker to indicate that it has been selected.

2 Press the Delete key, and click Yes to delete the relationship.

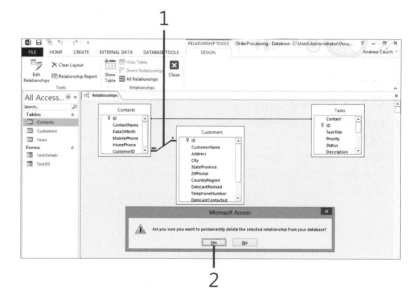

Adding relationships

Access is fantastic for importing data from other sources. After you've imported that data, you might want to create relationships to existing data. This helps ensure that when new data is entered, it is consistent. Access allows you to create two kinds of relationship. The first type simply joins two tables together and means that when you create queries, Access knows how to join the tables. This is indicated by a simple line between the two tables.

The second type of relationship is one that enforces referential integrity. This is a special relationship, which also has rules to ensure that the data in different tables is consistent.

Add a relationship

1 In the relationship design view, if the table is not already displayed in the diagram, click Show Table and select the table from the list of available tables.

2 Double-click the table name to add the table to the diagram (if not already displayed). Click Close to close the Show Table popup window.

(continued on next page)

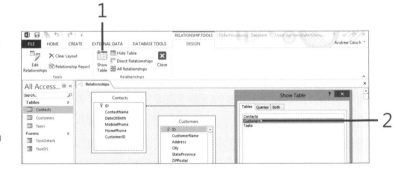

(continued on next page)

> ✅ **TIP** To create or edit relationships between tables in the relationship diagram, the tables must not be open in other tabs or windows. You should create the relationship between fields that are of the same data type. If you choose to enforce referential integrity, any existing data in a field that is part of the relationship must be consistent with the data on the other side of the relationship. For example, if we had in the Contacts table a CustomerID with a value of 99 but no record in the Customer table with ID 99, we could not enforce referential integrity.

Add a relationship *(continued)*

3 Click a field on one table.

4 Drag a field onto another table. The Edit Relationships popup window displays when you drop the field onto the other table.

5 Select the Enforce Referential Integrity check box.

6 Click Create.

7 We can see the new relationship line displayed on the diagram.

8 Click Save to save your relationship picture.

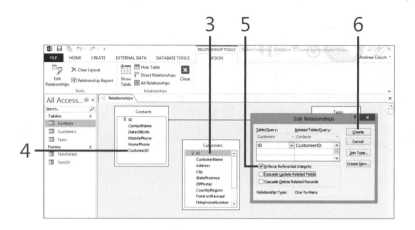

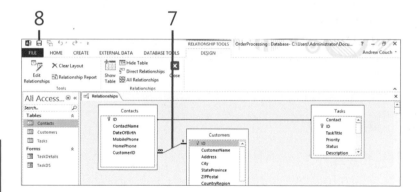

> ✓ **TIP** When a relationship enforces referential integrity, you will normally see a 1 at one end of the relationship and an infinity symbol (∞) at the other side of the relationship. In our diagram, you will see a relationship between the Contacts and Tasks table that does not have these symbols on the relationship line. This is because that relationship does not enforce referential integrity checking. Most databases do not have this ability to define relationships that might or might not have referential integrity. A relationship without referential integrity does not enforce rules but instead acts as a guide for how the tables can be tied together when queries are created.

Working with data in datasheets

5

A datasheet is a tabulation of your data (it can be based on a table or a query) through which you can insert, delete, and update data. The data can be filtered, searched, and sorted. But the humble datasheet offers a number of more sophisticated features, including drilling down to display related data in other tables or queries, using subdatasheets , and displaying summary information.

There are a large number of presentation features in a datasheet. You can change the layouts adjusting fonts; setting grid row height, column width, and colors; and by alternating row colors. When altered, the datasheet layouts can be saved and the datasheet remembers these settings when it is next opened.

In addition, you can reorder columns and filter rows of data to create areas of data that you can then copy to the clipboard and paste into other applications.

You can also switch forms to a Datasheet view, which makes the presentation capabilities of a datasheet an even more useful feature of Access.

In this section:

- Changing Access database options
- Moving between records and using Find And Replace
- Altering the presentation by ordering, hiding, and freezing fields
- Sorting and filtering datasheet rows
- Deleting, inserting, updating, and creating summary data for records
- Displaying related information with a subdatasheet
- Adjusting column/row height and formatting
- Selecting data to copy and paste
- Displaying more information with the Zoom box
- Changing the datasheet presentation

Changing Access database options

The database options screen enables you to make basic choices for controlling how you interact with your database, what you can do with it, and how data is presented. If you have received an application from another source or constructed a template that includes application program code, there are also some special considerations to give to these settings.

Because macros can be maliciously applied in applications, Microsoft by default disables their execution. However, in trusted applications, you will almost certainly want to enable some of these features. Most developers will choose to disable trusted locations and enable unsigned macro execution so that their applications can be used. The choice is yours.

Change the default database options

1 To allow macro execution when opening a database, click Enable Content.

2 To change the default options for the database, click the File tab.

3 Click Options.

4 Click Current Database.

5 Type a title for your application.

6 Decide whether you want an overlapping or a tabbed view. (We suggest that you experiment with both options to see which layout best suits your needs, using the two options under Document Window Options.)

7 Click Trust Center.

(continued on next page)

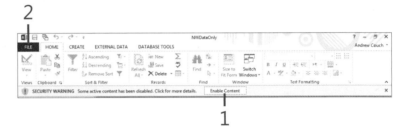

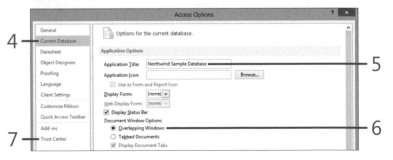

> **TIP** If you click the Enable Content button, the next time you open the database you will not need to do so again. However, if you use the file system to copy the file, rename the file, or move the file to a different location, you will be prompted again to enable the content.

Change the default database options *(continued)*

8 Click Trust Center Settings.

9 Click Macro Settings.

10 To allow the full features of macros, select the Enable All Macros check box, and click OK.

11 Click Trusted Locations.

12 To disable trusted locations when opening an application, select the Disable All Trusted Locations check box.

13 Click OK to close the Trust Center window, click OK to close the Access Options window, and then close and reopen your database.

8

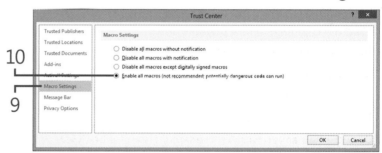

10

9

SEE ALSO For further advice on settings related to Trusted Documents when you are working with macro commands, you might also want to refer to Section 12, "Introducing the power of macros," starting on page 219.

TIP There are two aspects of trust that you can manage: first is the location of a file (Trusted Locations), and whether the application should be allowed to execute certain macro commands or VBA programming code.

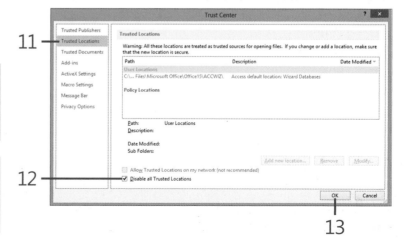

11

12

13

Altering the presentation by ordering, hiding, and freezing fields

A datasheet consists of a number of rows of data; the rows are composed of columns (or fields). Without actually changing the design of a table, you can manipulate the datasheet to reorder, hide, and freeze columns. (Even when you scroll the datasheet to the left or right, the frozen columns always remain in view.)

The ordering of the data rows is controlled by filtering and sorting, discussed in "Sorting datasheet rows" on page 77 and "Filtering datasheet rows" on page 78. Note that the terms *column* and *field* have the same meaning.

Order columns

1 Click the column heading.

2 Drag the column to a new position.

3 When closing the datasheet, click Yes to save the settings.

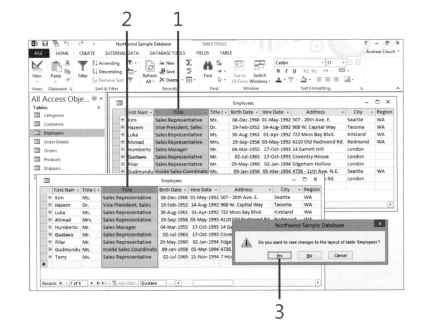

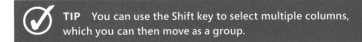

TIP   You can use the Shift key to select multiple columns, which you can then move as a group.

Hide and unhide columns

1 Right-click a column heading.

2 Select Hide Fields to hide the column.

3 Select Unhide Fields to display a full list of columns, which can then be hidden or unhidden.

4 In the Unhide Columns popup window, select the columns to hide or unhide, and click Close.

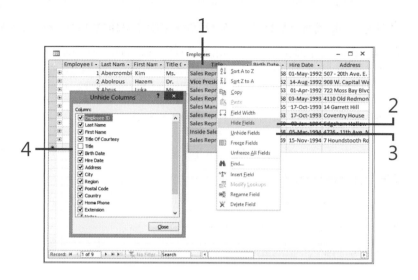

Freeze and unfreeze columns

1 Order your columns with the columns to freeze on the left.

2 Right-click the rightmost column, and select Freeze Fields.

3 To unfreeze all fields, right-click any column and selectUnfreeze All Fields.

> **TIP** After choosing to hide/unhide or freeze/unfreeze columns, when you close the table you will be prompted to save your changes. Doing so means that the datasheet will remember your choices.

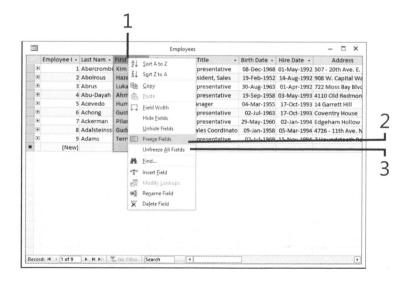

Moving between records and using Find And Replace

When you are working with datasheets and forms, the navigation control on the bottom left of a datasheet layout allows you to move forward and backward through the data, one record at a time, or move to the first or last record. The Record Number box also allows you to move directly to a specific record by typing the record number to be displayed.

Move between records

1 Click the forward icon to move to the next record.

2 Click the last record icon to move to the last record.

3 In the Record box, type a record number and press Enter to go to a specific record.

 TRY THIS   The PgUp and PgDn keys are also helpful when you are browsing through a list of records.

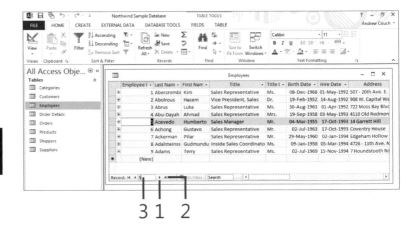

3 1 2

Search through records

1 Type a value in the Search box, and press Enter.

2 Press Ctrl+F to display more advanced searching options.

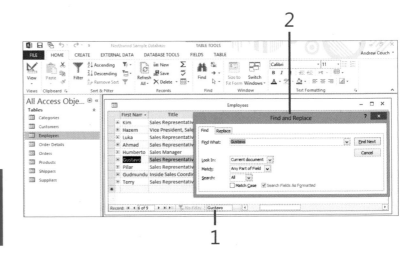

2

1

TIP   The Find And Replace option provides a number of more advanced searching features. For example, the Look In drop-down box allows you to focus a search in the specific column that you are working in.

Sorting datasheet rows

Access is a very powerful tool for filtering and sorting your data rows to show a subset of all available data. In Section 6, "Selecting data using queries," we will see how queries extend the ideas described here to offer support for even more flexible techniques.

With a datasheet, you can use the columns independently to sort the rows. The sorting order is always read from left to right, and sorting by multiple columns is supported.

Apply a sort on a column

1 Select the column.

2 Right-click the selected column, and on the shortcut menu, select either Sort A To Z or Sort Z To A.

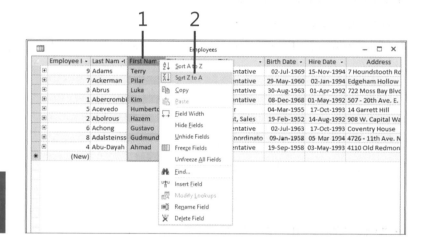

> ✓ **TIP** The sorting order of fields is applied from left to right, and fields for sorting do not need to be next to each other, although this can make it easier to perform a sort on multiple fields.

Remove a sort

1 Click Remove Sort on the ribbon.

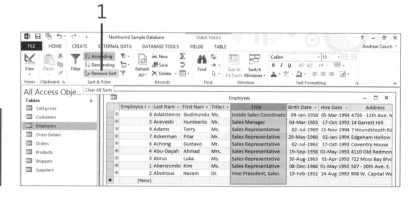

> ✓ **TIP** The shortcut menu does not have an option to remove a sort. When using the ribbon to remove the sort, you can see that it also supports options to apply an Ascending (A to Z) or Descending (Z to A) sort.

Filtering datasheet rows

While viewing a datasheet, you can filter information by using two techniques. The first method is to browse or search through the data until you reach a particular piece of information and then apply a filter based on the information you are displaying.

The second technique enables you to select one or more columns to display specific sets of records by clicking on a column heading. These headings then provide a drop-down list displaying the unique data values in the column.

Apply a filter on a column

1 Click any cell containing data.

2 Right-click the selected cell. (You have a large number of shortcut choices; the simplest is to filter by the selected value.)

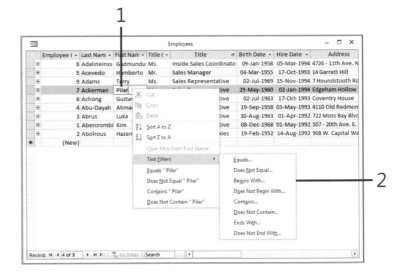

Remove a filter on a column

1   Click the Filtered button at the bottom of the datasheet.

Filter by column title bar

1   Click the column drop-down arrow.

2   Select the values you want to filter for.

3   Click OK.

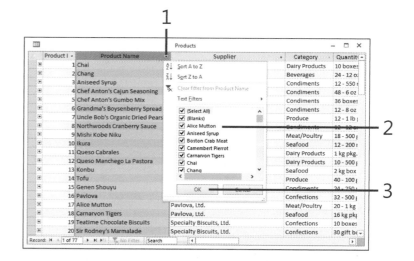

 TIP   You can repeat this operation for multiple columns to further filter your data.

Filtering combinations of choices with Filter By Form

The advanced filtering and sorting options provide two different ways to make selections for filtering: using the Advanced Filter/Sort option or using the Filter By Form option. You can save both filtering methods by using the Save As Query option and then reapply them by using the Load From Query option. We will discuss queries in Section 6, "Select data using queries."

The Filter By Form option is similar to Advanced Filter/Sort but offers more assistance, with drop-down boxes for selecting data values as well as presenting alternative criteria on separate pages.

Apply Filter By Form

1 Click Advanced Filter Options on the ribbon.

2 Select Filter By Form.

3 Either type criteria or use the drop-down list of values.

4 Use the Or tabs to enter additional criteria.

5 Click the Filter button to apply the filter.

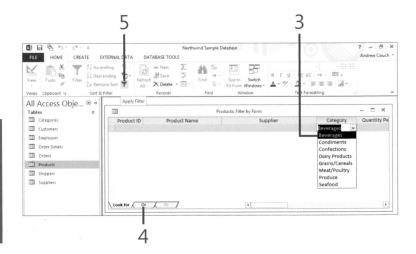

> ✓ **TIP**   Text can be shown beside the icons in the Sort & Filter group. This text can be hidden, depending on screen resolution (in our screen, it is hidden), and this can also depend on whether Access is set to use Overlapping Windows or Tabbed Documents, as described) in "Change the default database options" on page 72. You might see the additional text Toggle Filter next to the icon depending on your screen resolution.

Save a filter as a query

1 As previously described, select either Filter By Form or Advanced Filter/Sort from the Advanced Filter Options menu.

2 Click Advanced Filter Options again.

3 Click Save As Query.

4 Type a name for the query, and click OK.

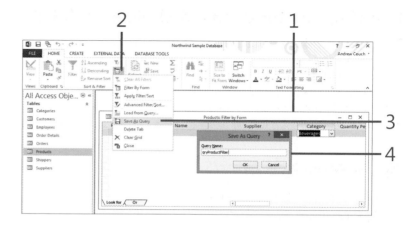

TIP When you enter text criteria, such as Beverages, you don't need to type the double quote marks around the text ("Beverages") because Access knows this is a text field and will add the double quotes. However, if you need to type a special character, such as an ampersand (&), as part of the data criteria, you will need to start by typing the quotation marks. Otherwise, Access can interpret the special character as an operation and produce "Baked Goods" & "Mixes," which is not the same as "Baked Goods & Mixes." This kind of problem is arises only when your data contains special characters.

SEE ALSO For a more comprehensive description of working with the filter grid, see Section 6, "Selecting data using queries," starting on page 95.

Filtering combinations of choices with Advanced Filter/Sort

The basic filtering option allows you to apply only a single set of filter criteria to data, but the more advanced options allow you to apply combinations of criteria—for example, when combining two different price criteria independently on two different product categories, you can examine how the product ranges compare against each other.

The advanced filtering and sorting options provide a more sophisticated method for controlling the display of the results. The interface used for defining these filters is very similar to the interface used to create queries.

Apply Advanced Filter/Sort

1 Click Advanced Filter Options on the ribbon.

2 Select Advanced Filter/Sort.

3 In the popup window, double-click (or simply drag) to add fields to filter by to the grid.

4 Type your filter criteria on each line, below the column name.

5 Right-click in the gray part of the screen.

6 Click Apply Filter/Sort.

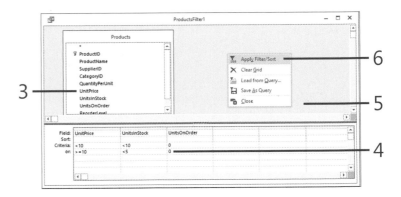

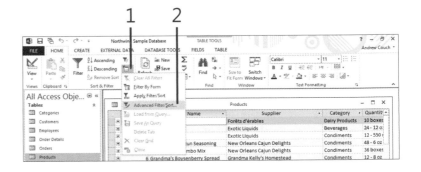

⚠️ **CAUTION** The ribbon drop-down item is called Advanced Filter Options, but one of those options is called Advanced Filter/Sort. It is easy to confuse these terms.

✓ **TIP** When working with either the Advanced Filter/Sort or Filter By Form option, you can save the filter as a query, and you can also load a filter from an existing query. These options are grayed out when you first use the Advanced Filter Options menu but are available after you have opened either Filter By Form or Advanced Filter/Sort.

Inserting and updating records

When you open a datasheet, you can normally edit the data by typing into a column. When you start to change a record, you will see a marker on the record indicating that the record is being edited. The Undo {Esc} key, when pressed once, will undo the current column value in the row you are changing. When pressed a second time, it will undo all changes made to the row.

To save changes to a record, you can perform one of the following actions: click the next field or record, close the datasheet, or press Shift+Enter.

Edit and then save and undo changes to a saved record

1 Start typing into any column in the row. (Notice how the record selector changes the symbol to a pencil, indicating that the record is being edited.)

2 Click in the next row; this will save the record.

3 Click the Undo icon. (This will undo changes made to the saved record.)

> ✓ TIP After you have saved a record the you can still undo changes by using the Undo icon, provided the datasheet has not been closed.

Insert a record

1 Click the New Blank Record icon, or click the last record, which is marked as (New).

2 Start typing into the row.

3 Click another record to save your changes.

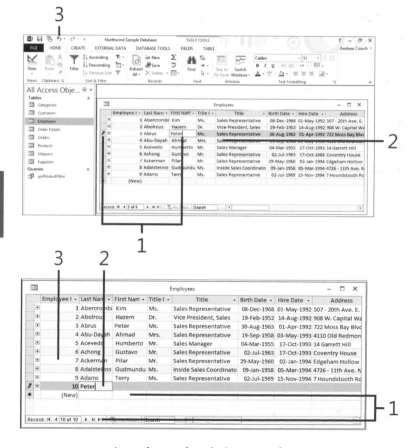

Deleting records

When deleting records, Access checks your relationships to ensure that you are not deleting data that would cause any inconsistencies in your database.

Delete a record

1 Click the record selector, and press Delete to delete the highlighted row.

2 In our example, the record cannot be deleted, and this results in a warning message. Click OK.

3 Click the expansion symbol (+) beside the record selector to show the related records.

(continued on next page)

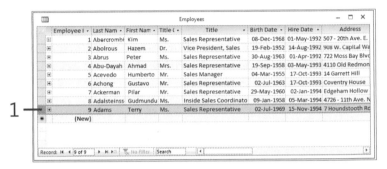

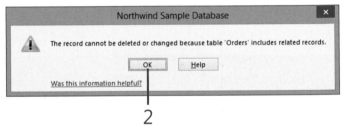

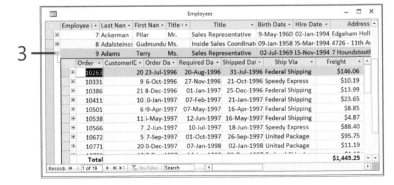

> **⚠ CAUTION** If you attempt to delete a record that has related records in child tables, depending on how you have set the relationship, either you will be unable to delete the record because the relationship prevents this or, if the relationship has a cascade delete, you will see a warning advising you that related data in other tables will be deleted.

Delete a record *(continued)*

4 Type a new record. This will have no related records.

5 Click another record to save the new record.

6 Click the record selector, and press Delete.

7 Click Yes to delete the record.

8 Working with a table that has cascade delete enabled in the relationship to related records, click the record selector and press Delete.

9 Click Yes to delete the parent and related records.

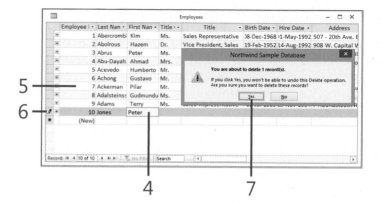

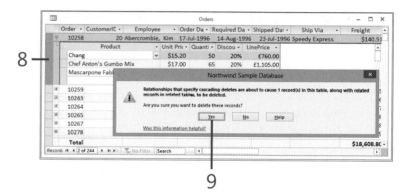

Creating summary data for records

A datasheet allows you to easily change the presentation to display summary data for any appropriate column, calculating a count of the records, sum total, average, maximum, minimum, variance, and standard deviation.

When you choose to close and save the changes to the datasheet, any summary totals will be redisplayed when you next open the datasheet. The summary calculations can be displayed both for a datasheet and any subdatasheet, which is described in the next example, "Displaying related information with a subdatasheet."

Display totals for a datasheet

1 Open a datasheet.

2 Click the Totals button. (This will add a new row for totals to your datasheet.)

3 In the new row, select the type of summary required for a column.

4 Save the datasheet.

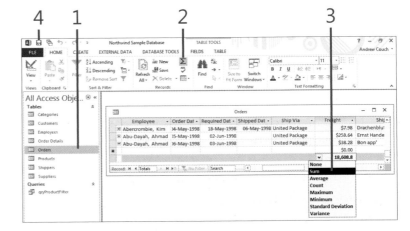

> **TIP** Notice that on the right of the record selector we have a plus sign. If you click this, it displays a *subdatasheet*, showing the detailed records related to each parent record. In our sample database, each Order record is related to several Order Details, and the Order Details are displayed as a subdatasheet. This very powerful feature of a datasheet allows you to drill down into associated details.

Displaying related information with a subdatasheet

Relationships are important to ensure data consistency. Access has a feature that can automatically provide you with drilldown capabilities to see the related data when viewing a datasheet. We use a select query in this example to show you features beyond the automatic settings. Details about how to create these queries are described in Section 6, "Selecting data using queries," starting on page 95.

When viewed in design mode, a datasheet (which applies to both a table and query), has a Subdatasheet property set either to [None] (which switches off the feature) or to [Auto] (which means that the relationships guide what is shown), or it can be changed to refer explicitly to a table or query. In our example we will use the query shown here as a subdatasheet.

Add a query as a subdatasheet to a table

1 In table design view, click Property Sheet to display the table properties.

2 Select the query to use as a subdatasheet.

3 Provide the appropriate values for Link Child Fields and Link Master Fields (linking key fields). If you have relationships, these might be automatically completed for you.

4 Click View, and save your changes when prompted.

5 Expand the subdatasheet.

6 Click the Totals button.

7 Select a Sum total for the LinePrice column.

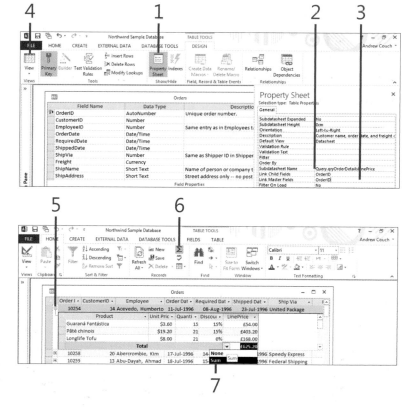

> **TIP** A datasheet can display only one subdatasheet. If the relationships imply that more than one subdatasheet could be applied and the Subdatasheet property is set to [Auto], you will be prompted to select which subdatasheet to use. The Access default behavior for creating tables is to set the subdatasheet name property to [Auto]. If you want to improve performance and not use this feature, set this to [None].

Adjusting column/row height and formatting

When viewing a datasheet, you will find that some presentation features, such as the font or color, apply to the entire row, while other features, such as alignment, apply to each individual column. There are two principal techniques that can be used to format datasheets. First, in the Access options, you can set a default style for all datasheets (the options here are fairly restrictive); second, you can tailor and adapt the presentation of an individual datasheet.

Adjust row height

1   Click the row, and drag down to the desired height.

 TIP   When the row is selected, right-click and select Row Height. This allows you to enter a numeric value for the row height.

Adjust column width

1   Click the column, and drag across to the desired width.

TIP   If you double-click the right edge of a column, it automatically resizes to display the data it contains.

Adjust row font

1   Click any of the text formatting options to change an aspect of the text.

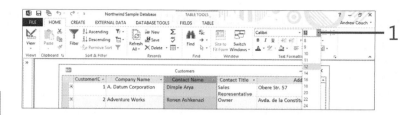

> ⚠ **CAUTION**   If you adjust the font, the change will be applied to both the row and the column.

Format rows and alternating rows

1   Click the Datasheet Formatting button.

2   Select the desired formatting options, and click OK.

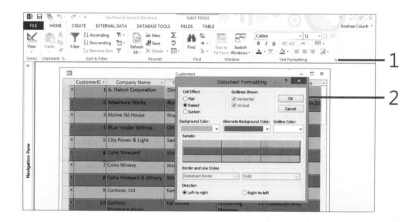

> ✓ **TIP**   Access also supports more sophisticated formatting, such as conditional formatting to color a cell to reflect the data value, but to use these features, you need to look at using a form to control the datasheet presentation (described in Section 8, "Improving presentations with forms" starting on page 129).

Selecting data to copy and paste

In addition to a very sophisticated set of features for exporting data, Access also supports a rich variety of techniques for highlighting and copying data to the clipboard. If you need to select multiple columns of data, drag the columns so that they are positioned together and then use the Shift key to select the columns to copy. If you need to select specific rows, use the filter/sort techniques to order the data, and then use the Shift key when selecting multiple rows or columns of data.

To select an area of the datasheet, click and hold as you drag the mouse over the screen area, having used the previously described techniques to order by row and column. To experiment with these techniques, paste the data into another Office application such as Word or Excel.

Select all displayed data

1 To select all data, click the top-left corner of the datasheet. Then use Ctrl+C to copy the data to the clipboard, and use Ctrl+V to paste the data into a spreadsheet.

Select a subset of all columns

1 Click to select the columns, either by using the Shift key or by holding the right mouse button down while you move over the columns. Then use Ctrl+C to copy the data to the clipboard, and use Ctrl+V to paste the data into a spreadsheet.

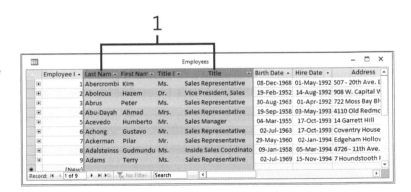

Select an area of data

1 Click a cell, and hold down the Shift key.

2 Move to another cell, and click once to select the area. Then use Ctrl+C to copy the data to the clipboard, and use Ctrl+V to paste the data into a spreadsheet.

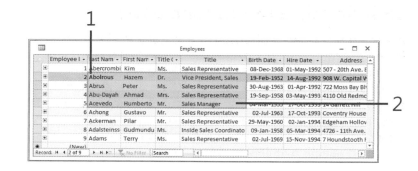

TIP Don't forget that Access has many other features for extracting data into other applications. These features are described in Section 11, "Exchanging data."

Displaying more information with the Zoom box

The Zoom box is useful when space on a layout is at a premium and you need to see all the information, or when you need to enter information that will be split over multiple lines.

The font option in the Zoom box also allows you to increase the font size to more clearly display the data.

Display information with a Zoom box

1 Click the desired field, and press Shift+F2.

2 In the Zoom box, click the Font button to adjust the font.

3 Press Ctrl+Enter to add a line break in the text.

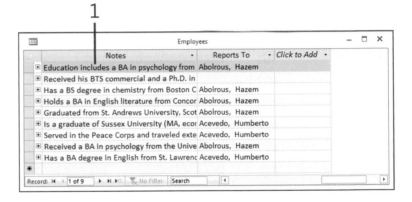

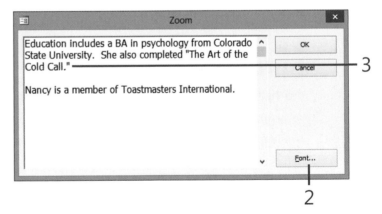

> **TIP** Within a large text field, pressing Ctrl+Enter will insert a new line of text. Also, if you change the font in the Zoom box, Access will remember the new font size when you next display the Zoom box, until the database is closed.

Changing the datasheet presentation

With the Access options, you can change the default font, font size, and presentation features of a datasheet to make working with the product more compatible with your personal requirements. You can then override these settings by making changes on an individual datasheet.

Change the datasheet options

1   Click the File tab, and select the Options menu item.

2   In the Access Options window, select Datasheet and adjust the default datasheet presentation to suit your needs.

Selecting data using queries

6

Queries are where a database can offer a real benefit over a spreadsheet because they allow you to construct sophisticated, updatable presentations of your data. These can vary in complexity from a simple filtered list based on a single table to more complicated presentations of summarized information involving many tables of data. Remember that a database encourages you to split your data into separate tables to reduce duplication of information when you are entering data, at the expense of having that data in several places. You will see that queries lie at the very heart of a database and allow you to reassemble the data from the different tables into a single view with greater flexibility than if the data were in one list.

The power of queries increases as you gain more experience with Access. For example, layering one query on top of another allows you to break down a complex problem into several simple steps. A query can display data both from tables and from other queries. Queries can also be parameterized to prompt users to enter filtering criteria, and they can be extended so that they are driven by selections that you make in forms. (See "Linking a form to a query" on page 224.)

In this section:

- Selecting all or individual columns from one or more tables
- Joining tables to see unmatched or missing records
- Filtering by single and multiple combinations of choices
- Adding calculations with the expression builder
- Returning top records and eliminating duplicate
- Creating a summary calculation
- Prompting to filter data with parameters
- Turning rows into columns with a crosstab query
- Working with queries that use other queries

Selecting all columns from a table

A query allows you to choose information from one or more sources, which could be either tables or other queries, and link your choices together to present your final results. The query design tool offers several methods for selecting your fields.

One key choice in how you construct a query is whether it will automatically include any new changes, such as adding new

fields to the underlying table. Using *TableName.** ensures that a query will include all fields from the underlying table, at the expense of being less efficient because it might include fields that you do not intend to use. However, if additional fields are later added to the underlying table, they will be shown automatically in the query results.

Select all columns from a table

1 Click the Create tab.

2 Click Query Design.

3 Click the table name in the Show Table popup window.

4 Click Add.

5 Close the Show Table popup window.

(continued on next page)

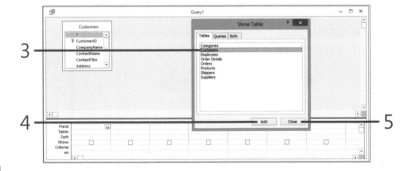

✓ **TIP** To return to design view while viewing the data in the datasheet, click the Design View option in the View button drop-down list. The View button allows you to switch between working on your design and displaying the results.

Select all columns from a table (continued)

6 Double-click the asterisk (*) to add all the columns to the query grid.

7 Click View, and select Datasheet View.

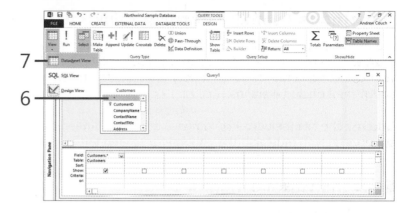

Selecting individual columns from one or more tables

Selecting individual columns has the advantage of enabling you to see exactly what is being selected. It also simplifies filtering and sorting because you can apply the criteria and sorting against the selected columns.

If you use the * to include all columns in a table and need to sort by a column, you must add the column for sorting to the query

(because you cannot sort against the *), but clear the check marks in the row titled Show when adding the column because you are already showing the column as part of the *, which selects all columns.

Select individual columns

1 In design view, double-click a column to add it to the grid (or drag it into the grid).

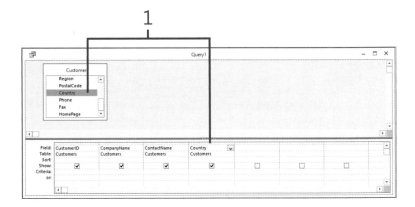

⚠ **CAUTION** Don't include the same field more than once. Otherwise, you are creating additional overhead. This can also create problems when you start to build forms and reports based on the query. The query automatically gives a new name to duplicated fields because each field name in a table or query must be unique.

✓ **TIP** To delete columns, click just above the column name on the column header and press Delete. You can insert columns by pressing the Insert key after you select a column header. The ribbon also has buttons to support these operations.

Sort by selected columns

1 Below one or more selected columns, choose either Ascending or Descending from the sorting drop-down list. To sort by a group of columns, put the columns in the order you want by dragging them as needed. Sorting is applied from left to right.

Join multiple tables

1 Click Show Table on the Design tab of the ribbon.

2 In the Show Table popup window, click a second related table to add to the query grid.

3 Click Add. (Note that the relationship is automatically shown in the grid.)

4 Click Close to close the Show Table popup window.

5 Select fields to display from more than one table.

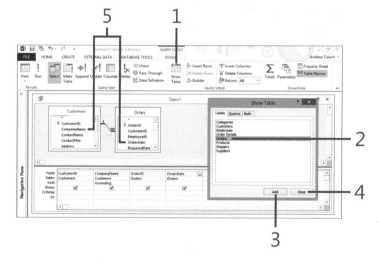

TIP If you have relationships in your database, Access will use these to join your tables. If your tables are not joined, you can click a field in one table and drag it onto another table to link the tables together. All tables shown on the query grid should be joined together. Otherwise, you will get all the rows from one table shown against every row from another table.

Joining tables to see unmatched or missing records

In "Join multiple tables" on page 99, we saw how to join more than one table on a query. Tables can be joined in one of three ways. The method of joining is shown on the diagram, with either no arrow or an arrow at one or the other end of the join. When you click the join, you will see a text description of how each choice will affect the data.

There are two classic uses of changing the join. The first allows you to identify unmatched child records (which can prevent you from creating relationships that enforce rule checking), and the second is useful when you appear to have missing records in the query results.

Find unmatched child records

1 Double-click the relationship.

2 In the Join Properties popup window, click the option to include all child records. (In this case, the Orders table is a child of the Customers table.) This will now show all orders, whether or not there is a customer in the Customers table for the corresponding ID recorded in the Orders table. Click OK to close the Join Properties popup window.

3 Add criteria to identify where the parent key (ID in Customers table) has no value (Is Null). This filters the query results to show only those records in the Orders table where there are no matching customers in the Customers table.

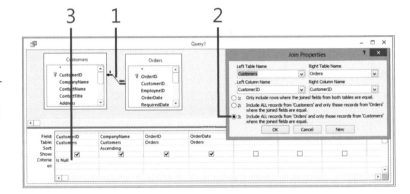

✓ **TIP** On the Create tab, you can create this type of query by using the Query Wizard, which will display a Find Unmatched Query option.

Display all parent records with and without child records

1 Double-click the relationship.

2 In the Join Properties popup window, click the option to include all parent records (from the Customers table).

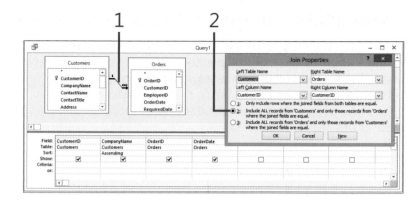

✓ **TIP** You can use this method to ensure that a report that has been created to use this query will display a list of all parent records, even when they do not have any child records.

Filtering by single and multiple combinations of choices

Each row in the query grid allows you to specify a combination of choices, which when taken together will limit the data displayed. Each line on the query grid allows you to specify a separate set of choices. This means that a query can apply very sophisticated sets of criteria to limit the data returned.

Choosing to restrict the data displayed in each column bases the matching on ranges of values, sets of values, and patterns in the data.

Filter to match similar text

1   In the criteria for a text field, type ***al***. Access changes this to Like "*al*", which will display any record containing the letters *al* as part of the data in this column.

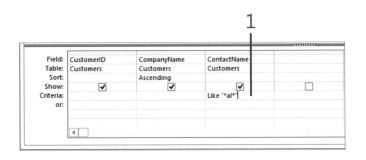

> ✓ **TIP**   Access uses the keyword *like* when matching part of the text in text fields. You do not need to type this because Access does it for you. Also note that searching is not case-sensitive.

Add a second set of criteria

1   In the query grid, in the Or row, add further criteria by typing **ba***. This displays all records where either the company name starts with the letters *ba* or the contact name includs the letters *al*.

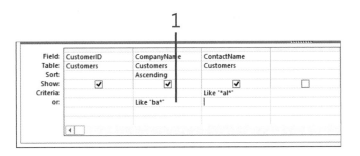

> ✓ **TIP**   If you add multiple criteria in each row, all the criteria in the row will apply. This means that we have an AND between the criteria; and between two rows, we have (row 1 criteria) OR (row 2 criteria).

Add a second set of criteria *(continued)*

The following table provides examples of using symbols in criteria to alter how data is matched.

Symbol	Example	Description
*	Like '*John' or Like 'John*' or Like '*John*'	Wildcard searching in text fields. You do not need to type Like.
#	#01/10/2012#	Matches a date. You do not need to type the pound (#) symbol.
BETWEEN	BETWEEN 1 and 4 BETWEEN #01/10/2012# AND #05/10/2012#	Number or date range comparison. Includes the first and last criteria.
IN	IN(1,22,44,55) IN('France','USA')	Set of data values.
<>, >, <, <=, >=,!=	> 25 < > 'France'	General and arithmetic comparison; <> and != both mean not equal to.
[?]	Like 'Fr[?]' Would match Fra, FrB, frC ...	Character pattern matching. Match any character (numbers and letters). Different from * in that [?] will include only records with only one character after 'Fr'. That is, it wouldn't return 'France'.
[#]	Like '000[#]' Would match 0001, 0002...	Character pattern match (0–9) for a single character.
[A-Z]	Like 'DNA[A-Z]' Would match DNAA, dnaB...	Character pattern match (A–Z) for a single character.

Adding calculations with the expression builder

You can type calculations in queries directly into the query, both to create a column and as criteria filtering against an existing column. To avoid mistakes when referring to field names or to explore the myriad built-in functions, you can use the expression builder to provide assistance when creating more complex expressions.

Access provides a wide range of built-in functions to help you create expressions. Two particularly popular functions are the *NZ* function, which converts a NULL to a value such as 0 for a number field or to an empty string for a text field, and the *IIF* function, which allows you to conditionally perform calculations. You will also find that the Zoom box is particularly useful when you are working with complex expressions.

Create an expression with the expression builder

1   Click a blank column heading. Make sure that you have already saved your query; otherwise, you will not see the column names in the expression builder.

2   Click Builder (or right-click and select Build).

3   In the Expression Builder dialog box, double-click the fields in the Expression Categories pane to add them to the expression.

4   Enter the functions between each field (such as *, +, -, and so on).

5   Click OK. The field expression will be read as
    Expr1:[Quantity]*[UnitPrice].

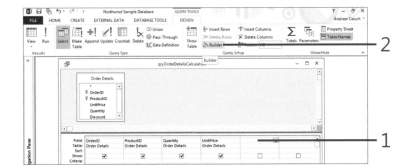

(continued on next page)

> ⚠ **CAUTION**   When you add a NULL value in an expression, Access makes the entire expression NULL. For example, in the following addition operation, 5 + NULL = NULL. This is where the *NZ* function is useful. In this case, it would convert the NULL to zero. So, rather than [Field1]+[Field2], we can use *Nz([Field1]) + Nz([Field2])*, which gives the result 5 + 0 = 5.

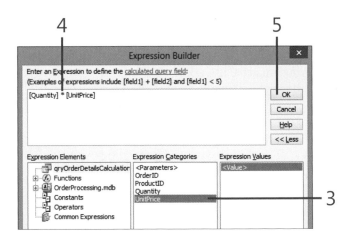

Create an expression with the expression builder *(continued)*

6 Click in the field, and press Shift+F2 (or right-click and select Zoom).

7 Edit the field title, and click OK.

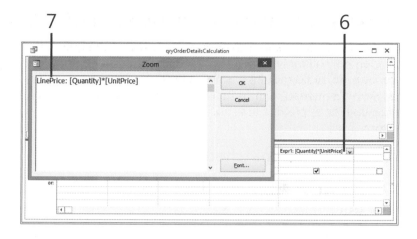

TIP All fields must have a unique title, even calculated fields that you create yourself. You can also use this feature to change a field name to be displayed with an alternative name in a query.

TIP When adding together strings (concatenating the strings—for example, [First Name] & " " & [Last Name]), use the & rather than a +, because the '&' prevents NULL values from making the result NULL. The '+' does not do this.

Returning the top matched records

If you order a set of results with a query, you might be interested in only a limited number of records—for example, the top five records, or the top 10% of records. A query has a Top Values property to give you control over the number of records being displayed.

Return the top matched records

1 Sort your data.

2 Click to select the number of records to show. You can enter values other than those shown in the list—for example, the top 3 records instead of the top 5.

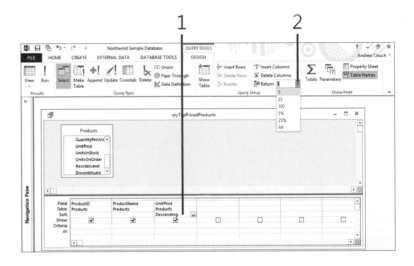

> **TIP** With our dataset, if we select the top 11 records, we actually see 12 records. This is because the top 11th and 12th records have the same value. Access always performs what is known as a TOP WITH TIES calculation, where records that tie for last place are always shown.

Eliminating duplicate values

Each row in a database table should contain unique and non-duplicated data. However, because using a query enables you to select only some of the fields, the values in those selected fields can be duplicated. This can be very useful when you are given a table of data from another source outside of Access and you want to identify a unique list of values in a particular field.

For our example, we have a list of Customer records where we have more than one customer in each city and we want to display a list of unique city names.

Eliminate duplicate rows

1 Select and optionally sort the field.

2 Eliminate any NULL values by typing Is Not Null in the criteria.

3 Click Property Sheet to display the Property Sheet, if it is not already shown. If your Property Sheet does not show the properties we have displayed, click anywhere on the gray background to see the query properties; the property sheet can display either query or field properties depending on where you last clicked in the query design tool.

4 Change the query property Unique Values to Yes.

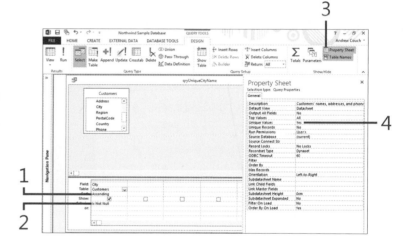

✓ **TIP** You can also find unique values by creating a summary query, where you create a query, select a single field, and then click the Totals button. By default, the field then uses a Group By Total, which produces an output similar to the method described here.

Creating a summary calculation

A summary query can be used to perform different summary calculations on your data. It supports the calculation of Sum, Max, Min, Avg, and other calculations.

After you have changed your query into a summary query, any new columns added to the query are displayed as the default

Group By values and group the data by that column. You can also change the Total row to Where, when you want to filter the data, or to a calculation such as Avg.

Add a summary

1 Click the Totals button.

2 Use Group By to group your results; you can add multiple fields.

3 Choose summary calculations.

4 Filter the records to summarize by using the Where selection.

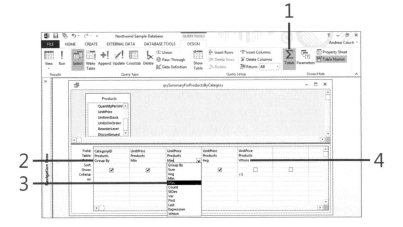

TIP You can put criteria against a Group By column to filter results, but it is more efficient to use the Where syntax because this applies the filter criteria to the records that go into the summary calculation. All other criteria are applied after the calculations have been performed, to restrict the displayed result.

Prompting to filter data with parameters

If you have a query that you regularly use with different criteria, rather than changing the design of the query each time you want to change the criteria or creating multiple copies of the query with different criteria, you can define a set of parameters so that when you open the query it automatically asks you to enter values for these parameters and then displays the appropriate data.

This type of query can be also used to provide data for a form or report. This means that you can have a report that, when opened, prompts for parameters before displaying the results.

Prompt with query parameters

1 Click Parameters.

2 Type a name for the parameter in square brackets. Ensure that the name is different from any column name in your query, or the parameter will not work.

3 Type a data type for the parameter, and click OK.

4 Type the parameter name without square brackets. IntelliSense will assist you here.

5 When you open this query, type a value for the parameter to see the restricted set of results.

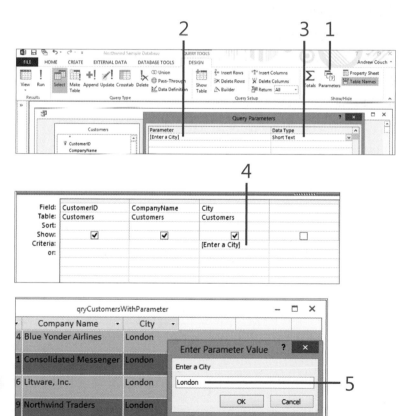

> ⊘ **TIP** When viewing a parameterized query in Datasheet view, pressing Shift+F9 enables you to enter different parameters and then refresh to display the new results.

> ⊘ **TIP** You can add wildcards to search with parameters—for example, by adding the criteria Like '*' & [Enter Product Name] & '*'. This is useful if you want to allow users to enter only a portion of the field contents rather than requiring them to enter an exact match.

Creating a crosstab query with the Query Wizard

Crosstab queries can be constructed manually. However, it is simpler to use the Query Wizard to create the query, which you can later change in design view.

Create a crosstab query

1 Click the Create tab.

2 Click Query Wizard.

3 In the New Query popup window, click Crosstab Query Wizard.

4 Click OK.

5 In the Crosstab Query Wizard, click Queries.

6 Select a query and click Next.

7 Select one or more columns to act as row headings, and click Next.

(continued on next page)

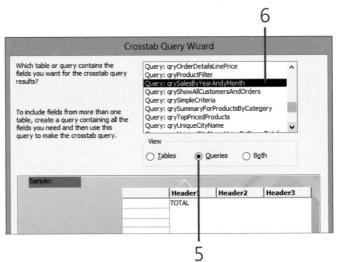

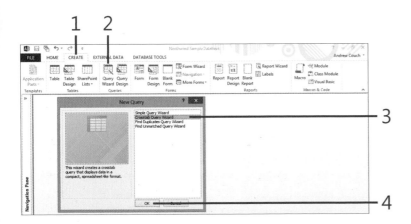

Create a crosstab query   *(continued)*

8 Select one column to act as the new column heading, and click Next.

9 Select the column to summarize.

10 Select the calculation type to use, and click Next.

11 Type a name for your query, and click Finish.

12 Select design view.

13 In the query Column Headings property field, type a fixed set of headings.

8

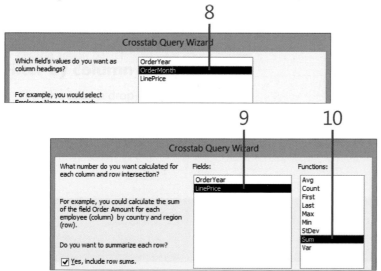

9   10

11

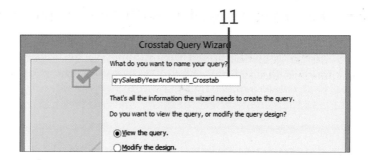

12

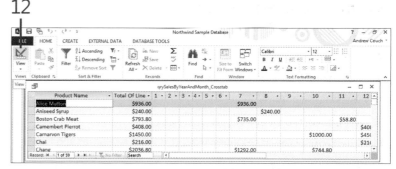

13

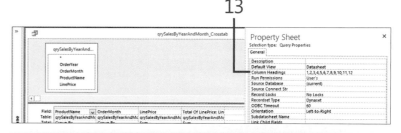

✅ **TIP**   The resulting crosstab query breaks down the orders received for each product into individual months (1–12), showing the sales of each product in each month in the month columns, with a row for each product. If new products and sales are added to the underlying tables, these will be included each time the crosstab query is run, adding new columns and rows as necessary.

✅ **TIP**   The column headings in a crosstab query are dynamic (for example, you could have only months 1,6, and 7), but you can fix these so that a column is always shown, even when it has no data. In the query properties, you will find a Column Headings property. In our example, setting that to a value of 1,2,3,4,5,6,7,8,9,10,11,12 ensures that we have a column heading for each month.

Simplifying a problem with a query by using other queries

If you have a complex problem—for example, you need to join together several tables and then perform summary operations—you might find it helpful to break down the problem into one or more steps. First, create a query that joins together and filters all the data, and then create a second query that uses the first

query as a source of data and performs the summary operations.

Using a query to work from other queries can also improve productivity by reusing other queries that you have already constructed.

Create a query to combine data from a table and query

1 In the design view of a new query, in the Show Table popup window, double-click the table to add it to the query grid.

2 Click the Queries tab in the Show Table popup window.

3 Double-click a query name to add to the query grid.

4 Click Close.

5 To join the table to the query, drag the ProductName field between the tables.

6 Double-click a field from the table.

7 Double-click the * on the query to add all columns from the query to the query grid.

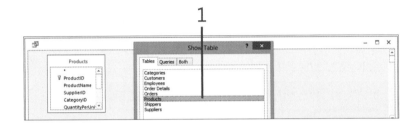

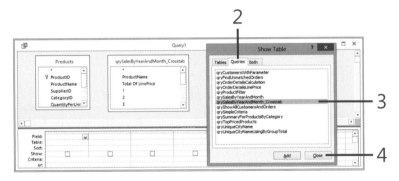

> **TIP** Ideally, when joining together sources of data, you should use primary and foreign keys, but in some circumstances you might be forced to join results together by other fields. When you are joining on other fields, the combination of fields should contain unique data values.

Adding two sets of query results together

When you have two or more sets of data that have the same number of columns, same column order, and similar column data types, and you want to combine them into a single list (although this cannot be graphically displayed), you can do so by creating a special type of query called a UNION query. This query uses a special keyword UNION (meaning bring together) or UNION ALL (meaning bring together and show duplicates).

You can combine multiple blocks of SQL with this keyword.

In our example, we have two tables, called Customers and OldCustomers, and we want to show the data in both tables in a single list.

Add two result sets together

1 In design view, add your first table to the query grid and display the desired fields.

2 Switch the query to SQL View.

3 Remove the semicolon (;) from the end of the SQL query, highlight the SQL query, and copy the SQL query to the clipboard.

4 On a new line, type the keyword **UNION**.

5 On a new line, paste in the copied SQL query, and change any references in the copied SQL query to refer to the second table and column names. The order of fields, number of fields, and data types should be identical in both sections of the SQL query. Field names can be different.

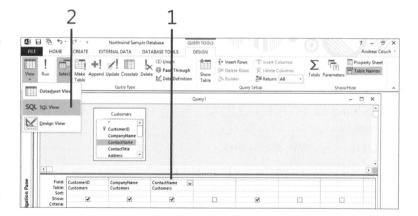

> ⚠️ **CAUTION** You are not allowed to select either Attachment data, Long Text data, or OLE data type columns in a UNION query. You can use the * to select all fields as long as none of the fields have one of these data types.

Resolving ambiguous outer joins

When you join tables together on a query and you have a line without any arrows at either end, you have an equally matched join (sometimes called an INNER JOIN or simply a JOIN). In the earlier parts of this section, we displayed unmatched records and missing parent records by adding an arrow at one end of the join; this is called an OUTER JOIN (being LEFT or RIGHT depending on which end all records are being displayed from). If you add tables to a query where you have already specified OUTER JOINS in the relationships, these will be shown by default when you add the tables to the query grid.

If you have a mixture of join types when you try to run a query, you will be warned that you have a join ambiguity, as shown here.

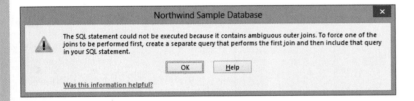

Creating an additional query to resolve a problem with mixed joins

We have a query that links together Orders, Order Details, and Products. Because we want to also show any Orders without Order Details, the join from Orders to Order Details is set to an outer join to include all Orders with or without Order Details. The join to products has been left as a matching join. This mixture causes a join ambiguity problem.

In our example, we could change the join between Order Details and Products to an outer join, but we want to demonstrate the solution that is proposed by the text in the join ambiguity warning box, where the query is changed to use another query that contains the outer join between Orders and Order Details.

Resolve join ambiguity

1 Click each of the tables where the join is different, and press Delete to remove the tables from the query.

2 Having created another query that joins together the tables we removed (with the outer join), add this query to the query design.

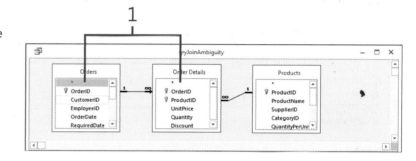

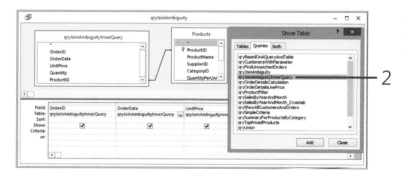

Modifying data using queries

7

The queries described in this section are a special type called *action queries*, which differ from the select queries previously discussed in that they are used to change data in the database. For example, rather than doing a search and replace, you can create a query to do that work for you. However, the power of these queries is greater than a simple search and replace because action queries can be based on data that you have in other tables in your database.

An example of a great use for action queries is when, after importing data from other systems into Access, you need to reorganize the data into existing or new tables. A Make Table query would enable you to create and add data to a new table and can be used to create new lookup lists of choices, or improve a design by splitting data into several new tables.

If you have a complex set of processing steps, then a Delete query could be used to empty tables, and then an Append query to repopulate the data, or an Update query used to modify data.

In this section:

- Creating a table by using a Make Table query
- Adding data to an existing table with an Append query
- Changing data in an existing table with an Update query
- Deleting data in tables with a Delete query
- Adding only new data that is not already in a table
- Updating a column based on an expression
- Resetting an AutoNumber with an Append query

Creating a table by using a Make Table query

The Make Table query creates a new table based upon the selections that you choose on the query grid. This type of query is useful when you are improving the design of a database by creating new lists of data or by splitting the data in one table into a set of tables.

In this example, we will split out a list of contacts from the Customers table to create a new table that allows the tables to record multiple contacts against each customer, improving the flexibility of the database design.

If you have imported data, you can run Make Table queries to move the imported data into new tables.

Create a table by using a Make Table query

1   Click the Create tab.

2   Click Query Design.

3   Add your tables and fields to the query grid.

(continued on next page)

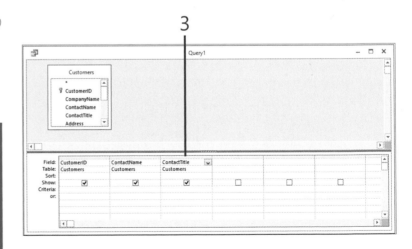

> ✓ **TIP**   When importing data, if you are repeating the import process on a regular basis and you have made other changes to the design of new tables created by a Make Table query, you might consider keeping any tables created during the processing of data, using a Delete query to empty a table, and then using an Append query to add in new data. This will prevent you from having to continue to use Make Table queries to re-create new tables and losing any other changes you made to the tables.

Create a table by using a Make Table query *(continued)*

4 Click Make Table.

5 Type a name for your new table.

6 Click OK. Before clicking the Run button, you can click View to review the data that will be created in the new table and then return to design view to execute the query by clicking the Run button.

7 Click Run to execute the action query.

8 Click Yes to create your new table.

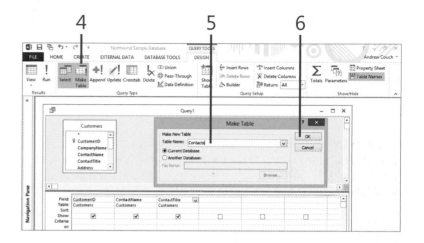

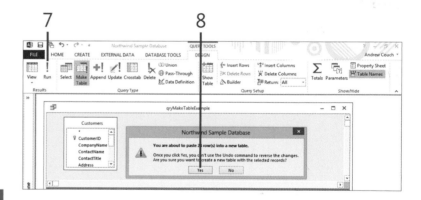

✓ **TIP** After you have provided the name for the new table, it is not displayed on the query grid. If you later want to check what the name is, switch to view the SQL.

✓ **TIP** After you have created a new table, you might want to alter the design of the table to add a primary key and set up any relationships.

Changing data in a table with an Update query

An Update query allows you to update the data in a table either by changing explicit values or by using data in other tables to help apply the changes. Update queries can also be executed to update data in a query rather than a table, as long as the query is updatable. (For example, a summary query is not updatable.)

In this example, we look at two techniques. In the first technique, we perform an update based on an explicit value. In the second technique, we perform an update based on data held in another table.

Change data based on explicit values

1 Start with a select query, and choose the fields to update.

2 On the Design tab, click Update.

3 Type any filter criteria and Update To values.

4 Click Run to execute the query.

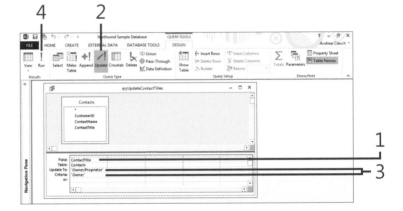

Change data based on data in another table

1 Start with a select query, and click Update.

2 Select the fields to be updated.

3 Type the name of the joined table and field. (IntelliSense will assist here.)

4 Click Run to execute the query.

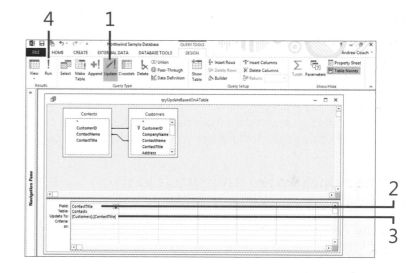

✓ **TIP** When running an action query that has been saved, you do not need to open the query in design view. If you double-click the query in the navigation window, it will run the query after asking you whether you're sure you want to proceed.

Adding data to an existing table with an Append query

Append queries enable you to select data from existing tables and add data into another table. Any rules or validation defined in the table into which the data is added are enforced when you try to append the data.

You are allowed to select data from several tables, but you can append only to a single table. After you have selected the target table, you can see the name of the table by viewing the SQL. (It is not shown on the query grid.) After you have selected the target table, fields where names match are automatically paired together; if the names are different, you can select the corresponding fields.

Add data to an existing table

1 Start with a select query including your table, select the fields to be used in the new table, and then click Append.

2 Select the table into which to append the data.

3 Click OK.

4 Use the drop-down list of available fields to match up any fields where the names are different. Where the names are the same, the Field and Append To rows will be matched.

5 Click Run.

6 Click Yes to add data to your table.

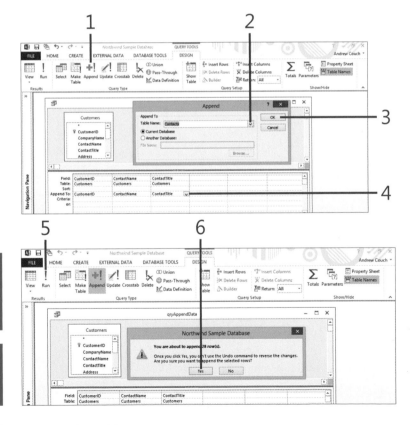

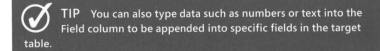
TIP Change the view of the query to Datasheet view to verify that the data to be appended is what you expect, and then you can return to design view to amend your query if required and continue to execute the query.

TIP You can also type data such as numbers or text into the Field column to be appended into specific fields in the target table.

Deleting data in tables with a Delete query

A Delete query allows you to delete data from a table either by specifying filtering criteria or by using data in other tables or queries to limit the data that is being deleted. As with all action queries, you cannot undo the operation, so making a backup of your database before you execute a Delete query is important.

Delete data in a table

1 Start with a select query including your table, and click Delete.

2 Select a field to filter the data.

3 Type the filter criteria.

4 Click Run.

5 Click Yes.

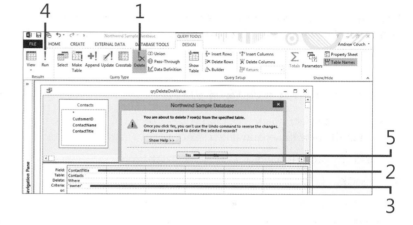

⚠ **CAUTION** When using Delete queries, always make sure that you add filter criteria to avoid deleting all the data. After any data is changed by the action queries, you cannot undo the changes. Making a backup copy of the database is recommended before you delete or otherwise modify your data.

Updating a column based on an expression

When working with action queries, you can use the data in other columns in the same table or data linked from other tables to change the data in the columns you want to edit. Examples include removing extra spaces from columns, splitting the data from a single column into multiple columns (for example, first and last names extracted from a ContactName column), or consolidating the data in several columns into a single column.

When constructing expressions, you can use a wide variety of built-in functions for manipulating data, such as the string functions UCASE, LCASE, RIGHT, LEFT, MID, TRIM, and InStr. In our example, we use functions to split a contact name into a first and last name.

Update a column based on an expression

1 To test your expressions, create a select query based on your table, as follows:

```
FN: Left(Trim([ContactName]),InStr(Trim([ContactName])," "))
and
LN: Mid(Trim([ContactName]),InStr(Trim([ContactName])," ")
+1,Len(Trim([ContactName]))).
```

2 Change the view to Datasheet view to check that all of the names are split as you are expecting, and then return to design view.

3 Click Update.

(continued on next page)

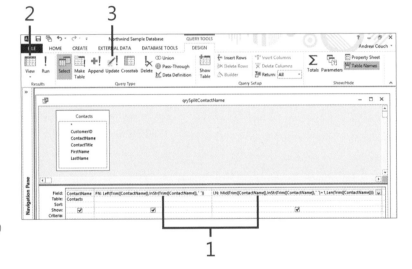

✓ **TIP** The Trim function removes any leading or trailing spaces; the Len function provides the length of the string; the Left function extracts the left side of the string; and the Mid function extracts the Mid part of the string. The Instr function is used to find the position of the first space in the string.

Update a column based on an expression

4 Add the fields to be updated.

5 Copy the expressions to the Update To line (removing any field title, such as FN:), and delete the old calculated columns.

6 Click Run.

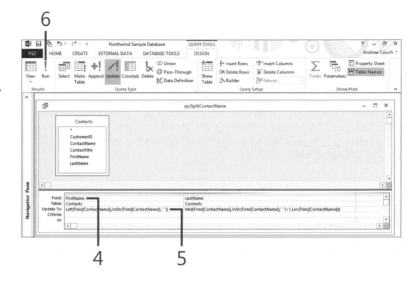

✓ **TIP** You should not be concerned when creating an update query that the final layout on the query grid looks significantly different to the original select query. The idea is to start with a select query to easily identify how calculations should be constructed, and then you remove the calculated columns using copy and paste for the expressions to transfer the calculation into the update to area on the grid below the appropriate fields to be updated (remembering to remove any labels such as FN:).

Adding only new data that is not already in a table

If you are importing data from a source table on a regular basis and you need to add that data to a table that might already include some of the imported data, you can use the properties of a join to ensure that you add only new records not already in the target table.

The technique is to have the target table not only appear as the table into which new rows will be added, but to also join that table to the table containing the imported data. Then you specify the join to include all records from the source table but to exclude those that are already matched in the target table.

Add only new data

1 Start with a select query, containing the source table, in our example Customers. Then Create an Append Query.

2 Specify the target table, and click OK.

3 Add the source table to the query grid. Our Customers table contains the data to be added to the Contacts table.

4 Join all the fields to be matched. In our example, these are the CustomerID, ContactName, and ContactTitle fields.

5 Set each join to include all the records from the source table (Customers), and double-click the joining line to display the join properties.

6 Choose one part of the joining fields from the target table.

7 Remove the field name to which it will append.

8 Add Is Null Criteria to the field. This limits the query to appending only new records.

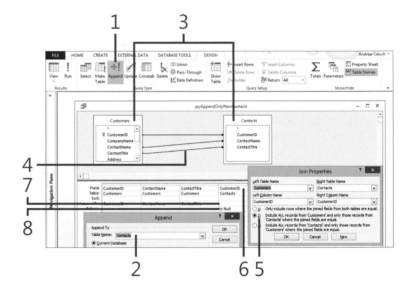

Resetting an AutoNumber with an Append query

Access automatically allocates AutoNumbers. Although they follow in sequence, gaps can occur when records are deleted. Also, if you compact and repair a database, it will reset the AutoNumber sequence to match the next largest AutoNumber in your table. That is, if you delete the largest AutoNumber, with a value of 555 (the next AutoNumber would be 556), and then compact and repair the database, the next AutoNumber will start counting from 555.

You can use the technique described here to either add back a missing number or reset the counting to start from a specific value—for example, when you want the numbering to start at a larger initial value. This involves creating a rather odd query that does not append from a table but instead appends a specific value into your target table.

Reset an AutoNumber

1 Start with a new query in design view, but click Close when prompted with Show Table. This will leave you with a blank query grid.

2 Click Append.

3 Select the table to which to append, and click OK.

4 Type a new value for the AutoNumber.

5 Select the AutoNumber field in the target table.

6 Run the query. This adds a new product with an ID of 9999, allowing new records to start counting at 10000. (You can delete the record 9999 later.)

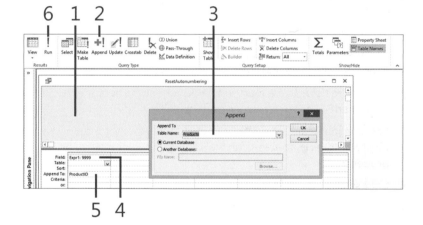

Improving presentations with forms

8

While a datasheet provides a flexible presentation of data, forms offer more sophisticated capabilities. Subject to certain rules, one form (a subform) can be embedded in another form and then they can be linked together such that when you page through records on the main form, only related information is displayed in the subform.

You can switch forms to present data as a datasheet, single record, or a continuous list of records. When you switch a form to Datasheet view, it offers extra features that extend a normal datasheet—for example, to use conditional formatting. Forms can display data from tables, SQL expressions, or queries.

A navigation form is a special form that you can use to organize the display of other forms; this allows you to create an application where a user can make menu selections to undertake different activities.

You can also display a form in form view, where you work with the data; layout view, which allows you to adjust the layout while viewing the data; or design view, which allows you to make more sophisticated adjustments to the form but does not display the data while you are making the design changes.

In this section:

- Creating continuous, datasheet, and split forms

- Working with form views and control layouts

- Creating a parent/child and a single record form with the Form Wizard

- Altering link master and link child fields

- Controlling editing and data entry in a form

- Changing the source of data for a form

- Organizing your database with a navigation form

- Adding fields to form in design and layout views

- Adding a subform to an existing form

Creating a continuous form with the multiple items template

The multiple items template enables you to create a continuous form displaying a tabulated list of records. When created, the form opens in layout view, which allows you to adjust formatting and other layout properties, such as row height, while viewing data presented in the form. This form is automatically given a tabular layout for the controls.

In layout view, the Form Layout Tools tab contains the following contextual tabs: Design, which allows you to manage fields and controls; Arrange, for altering the position of controls; and Format, for changing control formatting.

Create a multiple items form

1 Click to highlight a table in the navigation pane.

2 Click the Create tab.

3 Click on the More Forms drop-down arrow in the Forms group.

4 Click Multiple Items on the submenu.

(continued on next page)

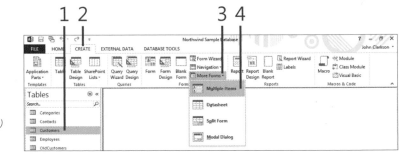

Create a multiple items form *(continued)*

5 Click the bottom of a row, and drag the row upward to decrease the row height.

6 Click to the right of any column, and drag the column edge to the left to decrease the column width.

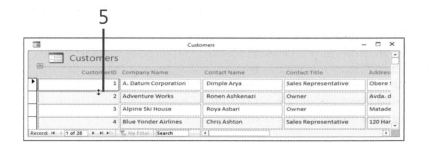

> ✓ **TIP** To move a column, click at any point in a column and then use the Select Column icon on the Arrange contextual tab to select the column. You can then drag the column to the left or right to reposition it. Make sure that you select both the column header and detail before moving the column so that you do not move only the column header or column detail.

Creating a datasheet form with conditional formatting

The More Forms datasheet template creates a form that is set to display the form in Datasheet view. In addition to using the standard features of a datasheet, such as dragging columns to the left or right or sorting using drop-down arrows from the column headers, you can take advantage of other formatting features, such as conditional formatting, when using this form.

Conditional formatting allows you create rules that alter the color and other format properties of a field, depending on the data it contains. This includes displaying a data bar showing the percentage of a value when compared to the total for the column.

Create a datasheet form

1 Click to highlight a table in the navigation pane.

2 Click the Create tab.

3 Click the More Forms drop-down arrow in the Forms group.

4 Click Datasheet on the submenu.

5 Click in a column to apply conditional formatting.

6 Click Conditional Formatting.

7 In the Conditional Formatting Rules Manager popup window, click New Rule.

(continued on next page)

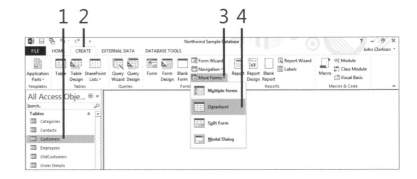

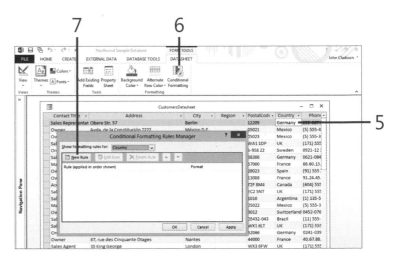

Create a datasheet form *(continued)*

8 In the New Formatting Rule popup window, select an expression.

9 Type a value for the comparison.

10 Change the background color for the rule.

11 Click OK to close the New Formatting Rule popup window, and then click OK to close the Conditional Formatting Rule Manager popup window.

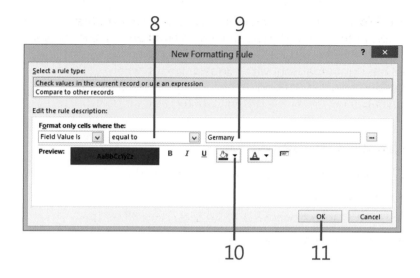

TIP If you view this form in design view, you will see that the controls are displayed in a stacked layout that does not look the same as the datasheet presentation. This is because the Datasheet view uses a special built-in presentation, and design view displays a layout that shows the fields to be included in the Datasheet view, not the actual datasheet presentation. You will also see that the form's Allow Form View property has been set to No, preventing this form from being switched to form view.

Creating a single record form with the Form Wizard

A single record form displays a columnar layout of fields for a single record, which means that you have more screen area available for your layout, but you can see only one record at a time. In comparison, with a tabular layout, where you often need to scroll left or right to see additional information.

You can use this type of form with one or more subforms to display data from related tables. (A continuous form cannot be used with subforms.) The form does not use a stacked layout for the controls, which means that you can position controls individually without moving them around on a fixed layout.

Create a single record form

1 Click the Create tab.

2 Click Form Wizard in the Forms group.

3 Select a table or query.

4 Select the fields to display.

5 Click Next.

6 Click Columnar.

7 Click Finish.

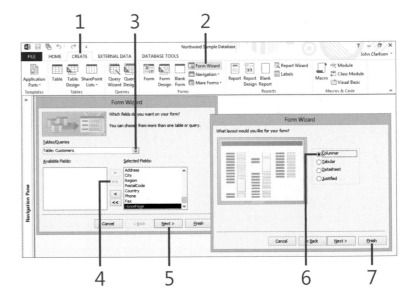

Creating a split form

A split form combines the single record form presentation in the top part of the screen with a datasheet presentation in the lower part of the screen. The two presentations are synchronized so that as you move to view a record in either area, the other area will update to display the same record in the alternative view.

Unlike the single record form, controls in this form are placed in a stacked layout. This makes it easy to adjust the presentation by using the layout view.

Create a single split form

1 Click to highlight a table in the navigation pane.

2 Click the Create tab.

3 Click the More Forms drop-down box in the Forms group.

4 Click Split Form on the submenu.

5 Click a record in the datasheet to see the corresponding single record displayed in the upper part of the form.

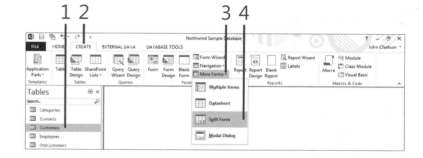

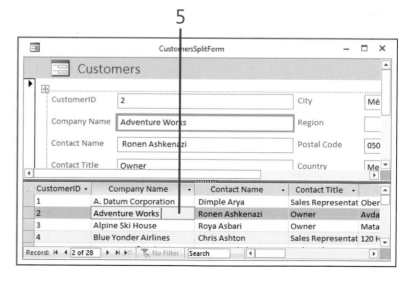

Working with form views

You can change forms between different presentations. The form has a property (which you can change in design view) called *Default View*. This property supports the options Single Form, Continuous Forms, Datasheet, and Split Form.

When a form is open, the choices on the Home tab for the View drop-down submenu will change depending on whether the default view is set to Datasheet or one of the other three choices. The following properties on the form further control these choices:

- Allow Form View

- Allow Datasheet View

- Allow Layout View

Change the default view

1 With a form open, select Design View. (The View drop-down submenu might be different from the example shown here, depending on the form properties.)

2 On the Design tab, click Property Sheet.

3 Select Form.

4 Click the Format tab.

5 Change the Default View property. To see the changed default presentation, close and save the form and then reopen the form from the navigation pane.

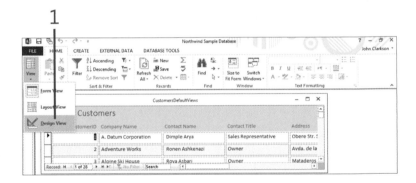

✓ **TIP** Although you can change the Default View property from Continuous Forms to Single Form, this controls only whether multiple or single records are displayed. You would still need to change the layout of the controls, moving controls to appropriate positions on the form to get the desired look for the presentation. A single form usually has both labels and controls in the detail section, while a continuous form usually has the labels in the header and the controls in the detail section. A great feature in Access is that you can mix these options together and come up with your own original presentations.

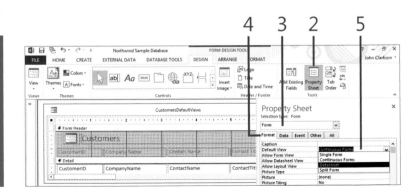

Working with control layouts

When working with the design of a form, you can either work in layout view, where having a control layout is an advantage, or in design view, where the layout can still be used but can be less productive if you are not used to working with it (because it restricts the positioning of the controls).

A form can have multiple control layouts. Each layout limits you in terms of where you can place controls, but it assists you by automatically presenting the controls within a tabulated layout. In this example, we show how to remove a control layout if you prefer not to work with this feature.

Remove a control layout

1 Click the Arrange tab.

2 Click a control in the layout.

3 Click Select Layout.

4 Click Remove layout.

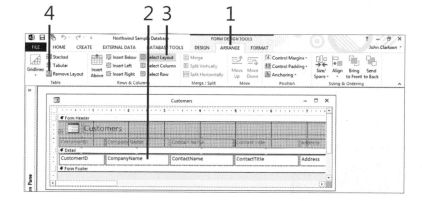

TIP With a continuous form, you can add a tabular layout, and with a single form you can add stacked layouts. To add a layout, select the controls by using the Shift key, and use the Stacked or Tabular buttons on the Arrange tab in the Table group.

Creating a parent/child form with the Form Wizard

Parent-child layouts allow the relationship between two tables (where a record in one table corresponds to multiple records in another table) to be represented with a subform embedded on the main (parent) form. As you move through the main form, the related records in the subform are automatically filtered by linking field properties on the subform control.

An alternative to a child subform presentation is to pop up a separate window displaying the related child records. You can create forms that use these features with the Form Wizard. The Form Wizard allows you to select fields from different tables and automatically creates an appropriate presentation.

Create a parent/child form with a subform

1 Click the Create tab.

2 Click Form Wizard in the Forms group.

3 Select the parent table.

4 Choose fields from the parent table.

5 Select the child table (which is related to the parent table).

6 Select fields from the child table.

7 Click Next.

(continued on next page)

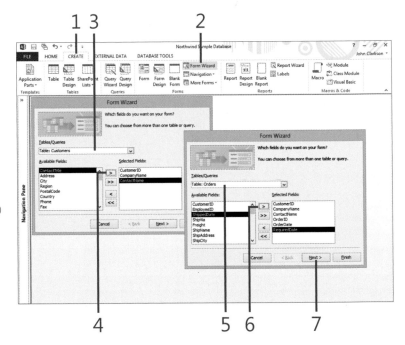

Create a parent/child form with a subform *(continued)*

8 Choose an appropriate grouping for the parent table.

9 Click Next.

10 Select the Datasheet presentation for the subform.

11 Click Next.

12 In the Form field, type a title for the parent form.

13 In the Subform field, type a title for the subform.

14 Click Finish.

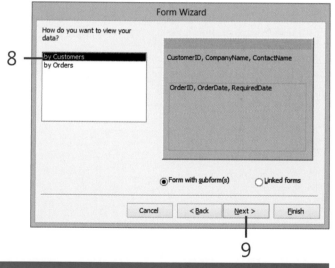

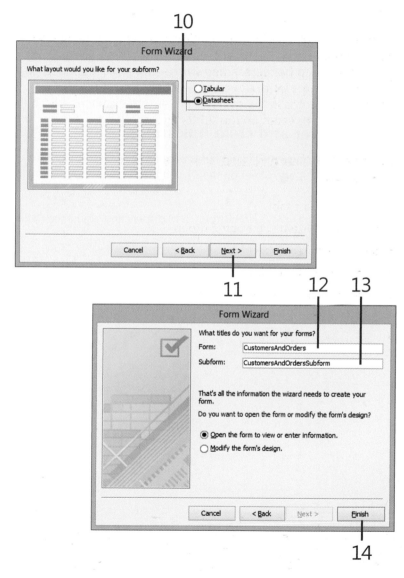

> ✓ **TIP** The names that you provide for the titles are used for the names of the parent form and child subform. If you name these so that the child form is easily identified with the parent form—for example, CustomersAndOrders and CustomersAndOrdersSubform—it will help you remember which subforms and main forms are used together.

Altering link master and link child fields

When displaying a form with a subform, if the child records are not being filtered as you move through the parent records, you will find that the linking master (parent) and child fields are missing and need to be specified.

In other situations, you might have added a subform that has automatically been linked to the main form, but now you want to remove or alter the links between the main form and the subform.

Alter master and child link fields

1 To view or change the linking fields between a main form and sub-form, click Property Sheet on the Design tab.

2 Click the subform control.

3 If necessary, use the build button (...) to display and adjust the fields linking the form to the subform.

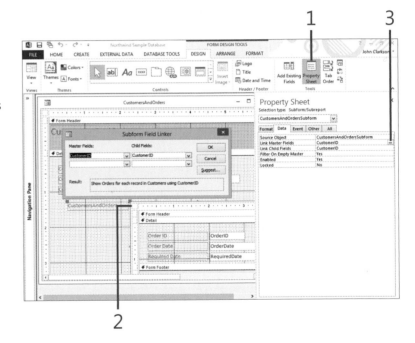

Controlling editing and data entry in a form

In form design mode, you can set a form's data properties to control whether data can be added, deleted, or updated on the form. Forms also have a special data entry mode, where each time the form is opened it is blank and, as you enter new records, only those new records are displayed in the form. This is useful when you are entering a batch of records.

You can also control whether a user can add new records (*Allow Additions* property), delete records (*Allow Deletions* property), and edit records (*Allow Edits* property) when viewing data in the form. These properties are located below the *Data Entry* property.

Change a form to data entry

1 Click the Design tab.

2 Click Property Sheet in the Tools group.

3 Select Form in the Selection Type drop-down list.

4 Click the Data tab.

5 Change the Data Entry property to Yes.

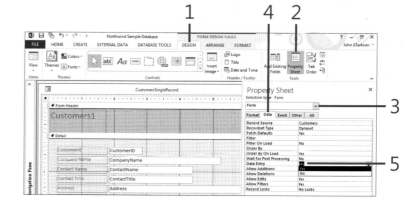

✓ TIP   Individual controls have a *Locked* property (Data properties) that prevents values from being entered or changed in the control and an *Enabled* property controlling whether a user can click the control. These properties allow you to set the Allow Edits property to Yes on the form but then restrict the individual controls that can be edited.

Changing the data source for a form

A form has a *Record Source* property that indicates the table or query providing the data for the form. You can change this property as long as the new source of data has the same set of field names that are used in the controls on the form.

In design view, if you start with a form created based on a table, you can use the build button to enter the query design view. From there, you can change the form's Record Source property

to a SQL string, which is then saved in the Record Source property of the form. You can then use the builder to edit this string to change the data displayed in the form.

Change the record source from a table to SQL

1   Click the Design tab.

2   Click Property Sheet in the Tools group.

3   Select Form in the Selection Type drop-down list.

4   Click the Data tab.

5   Click the build button (...) for the Record Source property.

6   Click Yes to open the Query Builder.

(continued on next page)

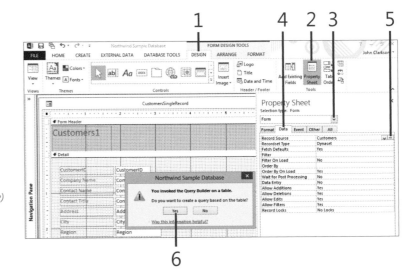

> **TIP**   If you already have another query that you want to use with the form, you can select it for the Record Source property, which can also display a drop-down list of tables and queries. However, you need to ensure that the field names contained in the new query include all of those used in the controls displayed on the form.

Change the record source from a table to SQL *(continued)*

7 Double-click the asterisk (*) in the table to select all fields (or select a list of the desired fields).

8 To filter by a field, double-click the field to add the field to the query grid, and then clear the Show check box below the field.

9 Click Close.

10 Click Yes to save your changes.

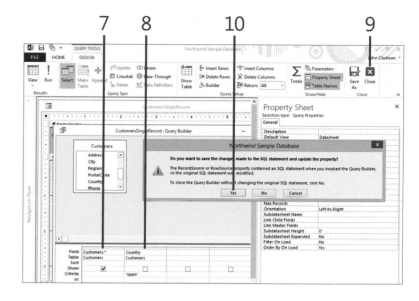

Organizing your database with navigation forms

A navigation form is a special form that allows you to create a form with a set of tabs that can display other forms or reports. (The reports will be displayed in report view.) You can open the form in layout view and drag other forms from the navigation pane onto the [Add New] area of the Navigation Form window to create additional links that will display the new forms inside the Navigation Form presentation.

Creating a two-level navigation form allows you to build a set of tabs with titles, which enables you to then group together forms and reports under each title. For example, a Customer Info tab could have a number of forms for displaying different views of customer information.

Create a navigation form

1 Click the Create tab.

2 Click the Navigation drop-down arrow in the Forms group.

3 Select Horizontal Tabs on the submenu.

4 Open the navigation pane by using the shutter bar.

5 Click to select a form.

6 Drag the form onto the Navigation Form next to the [Add New] tab. This will create a new tab for the selected form.

(continued on next page)

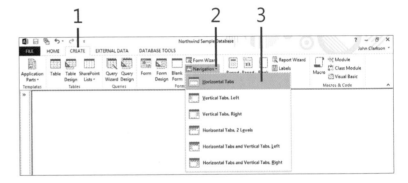

TIP If you choose to create a two-level navigation form, you can click in the [Add New] tab on the first level and type text. Clicking a tab in the first level then allows you to drag forms or reports onto the second-level tab, creating a hierarchy of tabs.

Create a navigation form *(continued)*

7 Repeating steps 1 through 4, but this time selecting Horizontal Tabs, 2 Levels from the Navigation submenu, double-click the [Add New] tab on the first level and type text for the top-level tab. Then proceed with steps 5 and 6 to add forms to the second level of tabs.

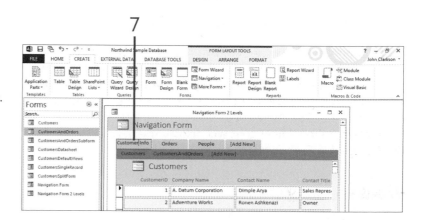

Adding fields to a form in design view

In form design, you can delete controls by selecting the control and pressing the Delete key. To add fields, you can drag selections from the Field List, which then adds the field control and label control to the form.

In a single record form, both the label and field control are added to the Detail section of the form. In a continuous form, however, after adding the field control, you need to move the label from the Detail section into the Form Header section.

Add a field to a single record form

1 Click Add Existing Fields in the Tools group on the Design tab.

2 Select the desired field to be added.

3 Drag the field onto the Detail section.

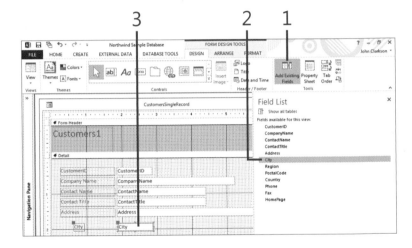

CAUTION   If your form is using a layout to group fields together (you can see this if you click a field and it is shown with a dashed outline around all the grouped fields), you should use the methods described in "Adding fields to a form in layout view" on page 148, or, alternatively, remove the layout before using the technique described here.

Add a field to a continuous form

1 Click Add Existing Fields in the Tools group on the Design tab.

2 Select the desired field to be added.

3 Drag the field onto the Detail section.

4 Cut the label from the Detail section, and paste the label into the Form Header section.

5 Adjust the position and size of the field in the Detail section.

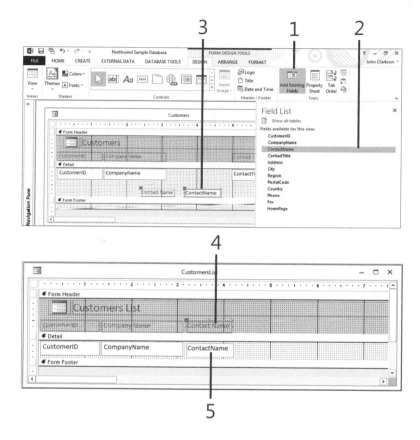

TIP In a single form, labels are normally attached to controls. If a label becomes detached from a control, cut the label to the clipboard, select the control, and then paste the label onto the control. This will reattach the label to the control.

Adding fields to a form in layout view

When adjusting a form by adding or deleting fields in layout view, it is important that you have your fields organized to use layout groups. These groups, which are added when a form is created (depending on the technique used to create the form, as described in previous tasks), provide a tabular or stacked layout for the controls.

There is a set of icons on the Form Layout Tools tab (on the Arrange context tab) that you should use when making changes to these layout groups of controls in layout view.

Add a field to a single record form

1 With the form displayed in layout view, click Add Existing Fields in the Tools group on the Design tab.

2 Select the desired field to be added.

3 Drag the field onto the Detail section.

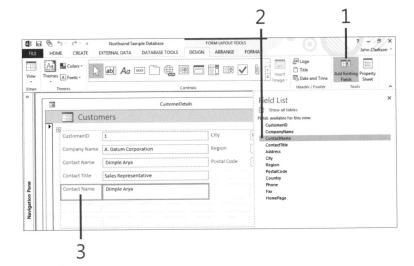

Add a field to a continuous form

1 Click Add Existing Fields in the Tools group on the Design tab.

2 Select the desired field to be added.

3 Drag the field onto the tabular layout.

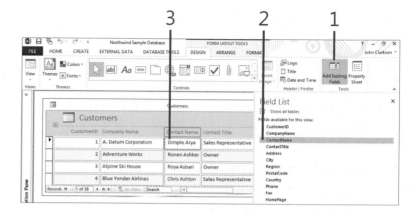

TIP On the Arrange tab, in the Rows And Columns group, you will find icons to insert spaces above, below, and to the right or left of a selected control. Often, using these icons makes it easier to create additional space when adjusting a layout to add new controls to a stacked layout (single record form). However, on a tabular layout (continuous form), it is easier to use the method shown here—that is, dragging a field onto the layout—which creates a new column.

Adding a subform to an existing form

If one form is opened in layout view or design view, you can drag another form from the navigation pane to position it as a subform of the first form.

When doing this, if you have relationships that define how the underlying sources of data are linked together, Access will complete the parent/child fields that link the parent form and subform together. Otherwise, you would need to manually defined them.

Add a subform in design view

1 With the main form open in design view, click a subform in the navigation pane.

2 Drag the form onto the Detail section of the parent form.

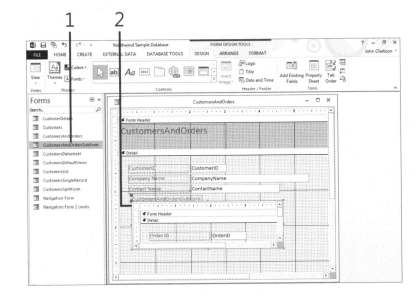

TIP If you try to drag a subform onto a continuous form, the form's default view will be changed to a single form, and you will be warned that you are not allowed to display a subform on a form displaying a continuous view.

Using controls effectively

9

When forms are created or when you add a field from the Field List pane to a form, Access will choose an appropriate control with which to display the data. However, you might want to change that choice of control. A simple example would be deciding whether to use a combo or list box.

A form that is based on a table or query is called a *bound form*. On a bound form, you can add either controls attached to your fields (bound controls) or controls to gather and present other information (unbound controls). It is also possible to have a blank form or dialog form, which is not bound, and on these types of forms, you can add only unbound controls.

The control box provides the Use Control Wizards (Default Selected) option, which assists you in configuring the control. To follow the steps in each exercise in this section, you should have this option selected.

In this section:

- Creating labels and text boxes, lines and rectangles, logos and titles
- Creating check boxes, option buttons, and toggle buttons
- Creating option groups, list boxes, and combo boxes
- Creating hyperlinks
- Creating bound and unbound object frames
- Creating image and web browser controls
- Creating attachments
- Working with tab controls
- Creating command buttons
- Setting control defaults
- Applying Office themes

Creating labels and text boxes

If you add a field from the Field List pane, the field is often displayed as a text box with an associated label (attached to the text box). You can add other unbound text boxes and labels from the label and text box controls.

Labels can be used to provide additional descriptive information, and text boxes can remain unbound, gathering choices made by a user, or can be bound to an existing field in the form's record source via the control's *Control Source* property.

Create a label and an unbound text box

1 On the Form Design Tools ribbon, click the Design tab with a form open in design view.

2 Click the label in the Controls toolbox.

3 Click in the form to position the label. You can then type text into the label.

4 Click the text box control.

5 Click in the form to position the control.

6 Click to select the label. Then click the label again to change the text in the label.

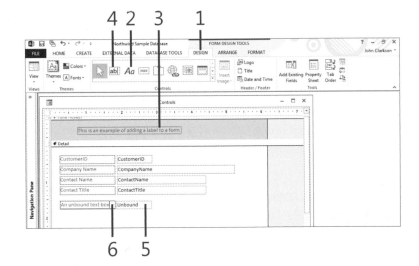

✓ **TIP** If you plan on later referring to the control by using macros or other programming, ensure that you change the Control Name property to something more meaningful than the default naming. For example, you could change a text box named Text0 to txtCustomerName.

Creating lines and rectangles

The control box contains a rectangle control and line control for marking out areas of your form's layout. If you want to create an area that looks like a grid, you can add a rectangle and then add lines to split the rectangle into several sections.

When drawing lines, you might find that you get better accuracy in obtaining a perfectly horizontal or vertical line by adjusting the *Width*, *Height*, *Top*, and *Left* properties of the control.

Create a line and a rectangle

1 On the Form Design Tools ribbon, click the Design tab with a form open in design view.

2 Click the rectangle button in the Controls toolbox.

3 Click the form, and drag across to size the rectangle.

4 Click the line control button.

5 Click the form to position the control, and drag across to draw the line.

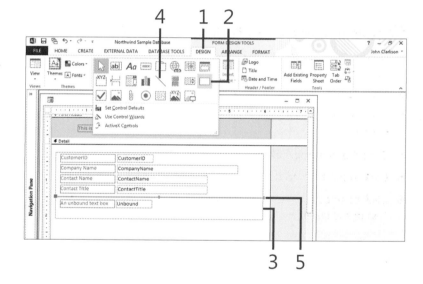

TIP   On the Format tab, in the Control Formatting group, use the shape fill and shape outline buttons to add color to areas and to change border styles for the controls.

Creating check boxes, option buttons, and toggle buttons

If you have a Yes/No field in your table, you can use a check box, option button, or toggle button to display and change the value in that field. If you drag a Yes/No field from the Field List pane, it will be displayed by default with a check box.

These controls operate independently of other similar controls on a form. If you want to have several check boxes that operate together, providing a set of choices from which only one choice can be made, you need to use an option group control.

Create an option button and toggle button

1 On the Form Design Tools ribbon, click the Design tab with a form open in design view.

2 Click Add Existing Fields.

3 Click the option button in the Controls toolbox.

4 Click a Yes/No field in the Field List pane.

5 Drag the field onto the form.

(continued on next page)

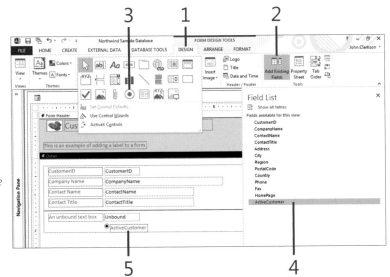

TIP If you want to add an unbound control, you can drag the control directly onto the form. For an unbound option button, check box, or toggle button, you would need to add macro programming code to make the controls perform an operation.

Create an option button and toggle button *(continued)*

6 Click the toggle button.

7 Click a Yes/No field in the Field List pane.

8 Drag the field onto the form. You might find that for a bound single selection, a check box or option button both work better than a toggle button. When combined with macro programming, a single toggle button can produce a nice effect to change the caption on the button.

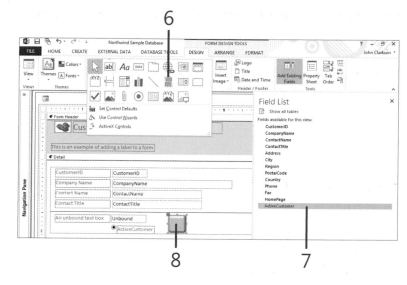

✅ **TIP** If you right-click the control and select Change To from the shortcut menu, you can select Option Button, Toggle Button, or Check Box. This process of quickly changing a control between compatible presentation types is called *control morphing*.

Creating option groups

An option group enables you to provide users with a set of choices from which they can select only one option. Each choice corresponds to a number that is stored in a numeric field in your table. (You can choose between a Byte, Integer, or Long Integer for the numerical data type to be stored.)

The option group also allows you to select one of the options as a default choice and to present options as a set of check boxes, option buttons, or toggle buttons. The Control Wizard will assist you in making these and other choices.

Create an option group

1. On the Form Design Tools ribbon, click the Design tab with a form open in design view.

2. Click the option group button in the Controls toolbox.

3. Click and hold the mouse at a suitable position on the form.

4. Drag the mouse across an area to size the control.

5. Type your option choices in the Option Group Wizard, and click Next.

6. Optionally, specify a default choice, by selecting from the available options, and then click Next.

(continued on next page)

> **TIP** If you need to add more options to an existing option group, you can either use the controls to drop a new control onto the option group or use copy and paste with an existing option in a group. In both cases, you need to check that the new option has a different *Option Value* property for existing options and that the option is part of the group. (Click the group to highlight all the options inside the group.)

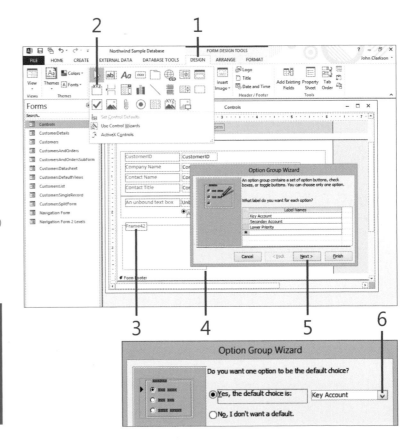

Create an option group   *(continued)*

7 For each option, type the appropriate information in the Label Names and Values columns and click Next.

8 Click Store The Value In This Field.

9 From the drop-down list, select the field in which to store the value, and then click Next.

10 Make any changes to the control type to display.

11 Make any changes to the control style, and click Next.

12 Type a caption for the option group, and click Finish.

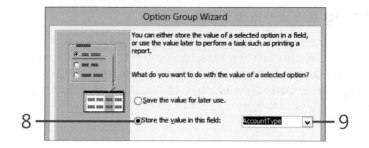

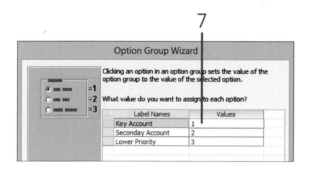

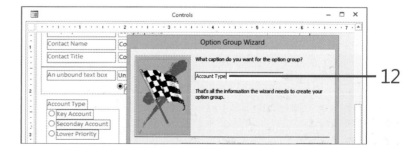

Creating list boxes

List boxes are a great choice of control when there are, for example, 10–20 options. You can configure list boxes through properties to allow multiple selections to be made. (For this, you need either an unbound list box or a multivalue field in your table.)

Both list and combo boxes can display choices that you enter when designing the control as a list of values, or they can look up values from a table or query. In this example, we show how to create a list box based on a set of supplied values.

Create a list box based on values

1 On the Form Design Tools ribbon, click the Design tab with a form open in design view.

2 Click the list box button in the Controls toolbox.

3 Click and hold the mouse at a suitable position on the form.

4 Drag the mouse across an area to size the control.

5 Click I Will Type In The Values That I Want, and click Next.

6 Type 2 for the number of columns.

7 Type choices for both columns, and click Next.

(continued on next page)

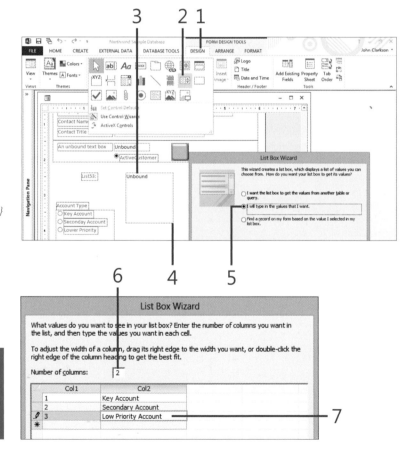

TIP When working with combo boxes and list boxes, you might decide to use two columns, where the first column will contain the value to be saved and the second column will provide a text description of the value. List boxes are often used to display multiple columns of information.

Create a list box based on values (continued)

8 Select Col1 to be the value saved, and click Next.

9 Click Store That Value In This Field.

10 Select a field from the drop-down list, and click Next.

11 Type a label for the field, and click Finish. (The form is shown here in form view with the completed list box.)

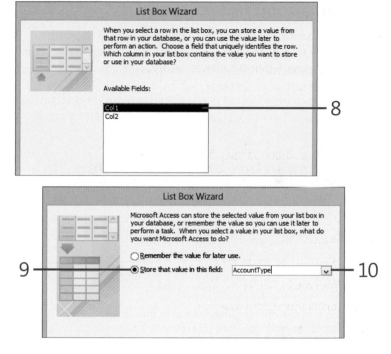

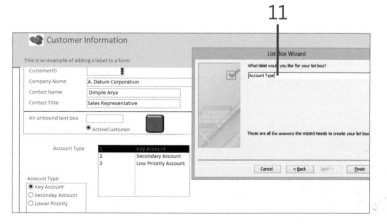

TIP In the design of a table, you can specify that a field is displayed as a list or combo box in the field properties. This can be based either on data in a table or on a set of values. Specifying the display type and values for the field in the table design means that if you drag the field from the Field List pane or use a wizard to create a form, the field will be displayed using the appropriate control type; this saves you a lot of time when laying out forms.

Creating combo boxes

As an alternative to the preceding example, where the control displayed a set of fixed values, the values in a combo or list box can be taken from either a table or query.

Using a table or query has an advantage over creating a control by using an explicit set of values because, in the latter case, if

you needed to change the values, you would have to make the change on all forms that used the control containing the fixed values. However, with data from a table or query, the current available choices are always displayed.

Create a combo box based on a table

1 On the Form Design Tools ribbon, click the Design tab with a form open in design view.

2 Click the combo box button in the Controls toolbox.

3 Click to position the control on the form.

4 Select the default option to get values from a table or query, and then click Next.

5 Select the table containing the data, and then click Next.

(continued on next page)

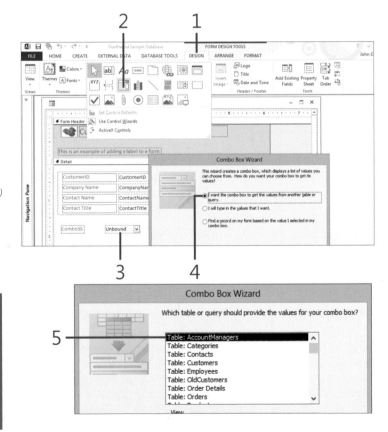

⊘ TIP As a result of your choices in the Combo Box Wizard, several key properties are set on the combo box control that you can subsequently change. For example, in the Format properties, *Column Count* is the number of columns, *Column Widths* is the width of each column (0 is for a hidden column), and *List Rows* is the number of rows in the drop-down box. The *Column Heads* property controls whether column headers are shown, and in the Data properties, *Limit To List* restricts entries to values in the list.

Create a combo box based on a table *(continued)*

6 Choose the required fields to use. (In our example, we have a numerical ID field, which is the value to be saved, and a text description field, which is the value to be shown.) Click Next. On the next screen choose a field to sort the choices, and click Next.

7 Accept the default to hide the key column, and click Next.

8 Click Store That Value In This Field.

9 Select the database field from the drop-down list, and click Next. On the next screen provide a caption for the control, and click Finish.

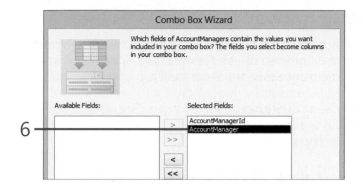

6

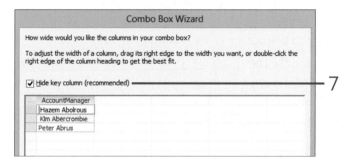

7

8   9

> **TIP** A combo box can display a drop-down list of multiple columns but can display only one of the columns as selected. If you need to show data from more than one column, you can use a query to create a calculated column combining the values from several fields.

Creating hyperlinks

A hyperlink control can display data that is stored in a hyperlink data type in a table. To use this feature, you drag the hyperlink data type field onto the form from the Field List pane, and the field is then automatically displayed via a hyperlink control.

In this example, we show how you can add an unbound hyperlink, which has a fixed value and can be linked to an existing file, a webpage, an object in the database, or an email address.

Create a hyperlink

1 On the Form Design Tools ribbon, click the Design tab with a form open in design view.

2 Click the hyperlink button in the Controls toolbox.

3 Browse to locate the document.

4 Click OK. The control is automatically added to the form.

5 Reposition the hyperlink control on the form.

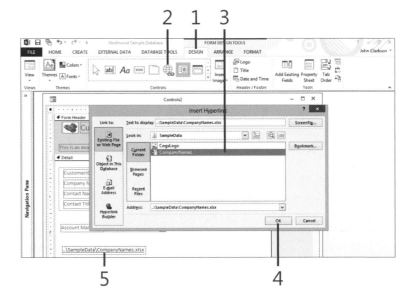

> ✓ **TIP** When creating a hyperlink, if you choose Objects In This Database (on the left side of the popup window), you can create a navigation interface using hyperlinks to other objects such as tables, queries, forms, and reports in the database.

Creating logos and titles

There is a button on the ribbon that you can use to add a title to your form. Clicking this button adds a label control onto the Form Header section, using a stacked layout, which creates two cells. The second cell will contain a label control that you can use to provide a title for your form. The first cell is blank, and you can use the Logo button (which adds an image control to the form) to add an image in this cell.

The shared stacked layout used for both these controls means that it does not matter whether you first add the logo or the title; you will get the same result.

Create a logo and title

1   On the Form Design Tools ribbon, click the Design tab with a form open in design view.

2   Click the Logo button.

3   Browse to locate the file, and click OK.

4   Click the Title button.

5   Type text for your title into the label control.

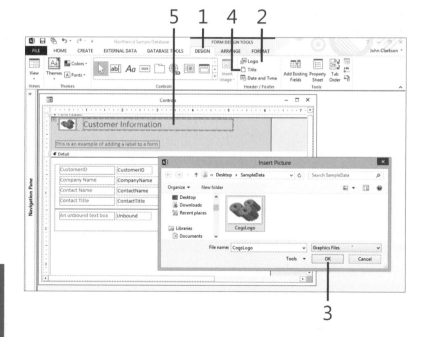

> **TIP**   Using this technique to add a logo to several forms will create a separate embedded copy of the image on each form. (It is a good idea to check and reduce the size of an image file before adding it to a form.) If you have a large image, you can use the Image Gallery described in "Create an image with the Image Gallery" on page 167 to add a shared image, which will reduce the storage required in the database for any images.

Creating bound and unbound object frames

A bound object frame is used to display an OLE Object data type. These data types allow you store objects such as spreadsheets, word documents, or images in your database. OLE Object data types were one of the first data types in Access for storing objects such as images. Access also supports a newer Attachment data type for storing similar documents, which has

the advantage of storing multiple documents on each record.

An unbound object frame can contain an embedded object (held on the form), or it can be linked to an object held in another location external to Access.

Create a bound object frame

1 On the Form Design Tools ribbon, click the Design tab with a form open in design view.

2 Click Property Sheet to display the Property Sheet pane.

3 Click the bound object frame button in the Controls toolbox.

4 Position the control on the form.

5 In the Property Sheet pane, set the control source to an existing OLE Object data type field.

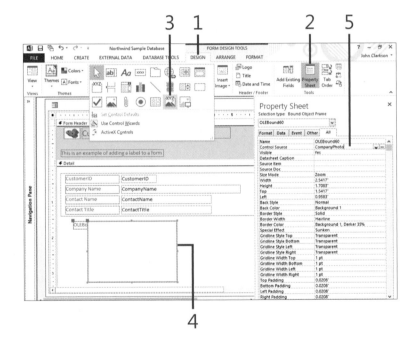

✓ **TIP** You can also drag an OLE Object data type field onto the form from the Field List pane. It will then automatically be displayed using the bound object frame.

Create an unbound object frame

1 On the Form Design Tools ribbon, click the Design tab with a form open in design view.

2 Click the unbound object frame button in the Controls toolbox.

3 Position the control on the form. (A popup window enables you to select or create an object.)

4 Click Create From File.

5 Click Browse, and locate the file.

6 Click OK. (The object is now displayed on the form.)

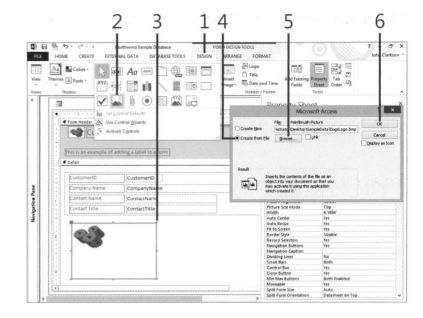

Creating image controls

An image control is used to display an embedded, linked, or shared image. You can add an image control from the Controls toolbox or by using the image button on the ribbon.

If you use the image button, the image will also be available from the drop-down list of images to be added to other forms and reports. The advantage of this approach is that the image is actually held only once inside the database, so you minimize the amount of storage used in your database, especially if you have a large image file.

Create an image with the image control

1 On the Form Design Tools ribbon, click the Design tab with a form open in design view.

2 Click the image button in the Controls toolbox.

3 Place the control on the form.

4 In the Insert Picture popup window, select the image and click OK.

TIP   If you examine the *Picture Type* property of the control, you will see that it is embedded (meaning that a copy of the image is held on the form). Other Picture Type property options include *linked*, where the image is held external to the database as a file, and *shared*, where the image is held inside the database but shared from a single copy.

Create an image with the Image Gallery

1 On the Form Design Tools ribbon, click the Design tab with a form open in design view.

2 Click Insert Image.

3 Click Browse.

4 Change the filter to All Files.

5 Click the file and click OK. This will create a shared image.

6 Position the image on the form.

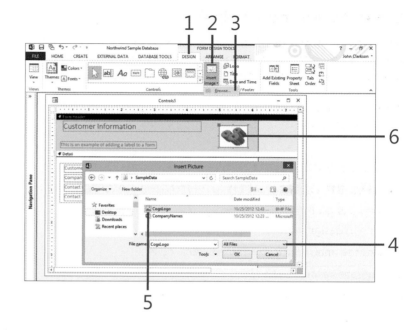

✓ **TIP** When you subsequently click Insert Image, Access will display an Image Gallery showing images already added to your database. This feature is available only in desktop .accdb format files and not the older .mdb format files, where the Insert Image button will be grayed out and not available.

Creating attachments

An attachment control is used to display objects that are stored as attachments in your table. Each attachment field can store multiple documents. When displaying an attachment field, the control displays the first attachment stored in the field and allows you to select other attachments.

We have shown the attachment control in the Controls toolbox, but it would be quite unusual to add an attachment directly by using the control (unless you needed an unbound attachment field, which would require significant programming). To add an attachment, you would usually drag it from the Field List pane as described here.

Create an attachment

1 On the Form Design Tools ribbon, click the Design tab with a form open in design view.

2 In the Tools section, click Add Existing Fields.

3 Select an attachment data type field.

4 Drag the field onto the form.

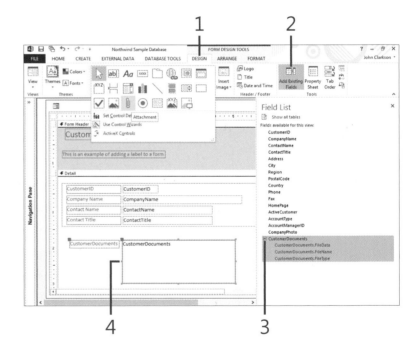

TIP   When you are viewing data through the form, if you load an image into an attachment, the attachment control displays the image. For other document types, the control displays an icon, which you can then open to display the document.

Creating web browser controls

A web browser control enables you to embed a frame that can work as a web browser inside your form (although without all the features normally found in a web browser). If you have the Control Wizards activated in the Controls toolbox, you can use the Insert Hyperlink popup window to display the results of a fixed webpage on your form. (You can change this later by clicking the build button for the control's *Control Source* property.)

The Control Source property for the web browser control can also be set to a hyperlink field in a database table—for example, a customer's home page. Then, when you display the customer record, the home page will be displayed in the web browser control.

Create a web browser control

1 On the Form Design Tools ribbon, click the Design tab.

2 In the Tools section, click Property Sheet.

3 Click the web browser control button.

4 Position the control on the form.

5 Click Cancel on the Insert Hyperlink popup window (if you have the Use Control Wizards selected for your controls). Set the Control Source property for the web browser control to a hyperlink field in your database table.

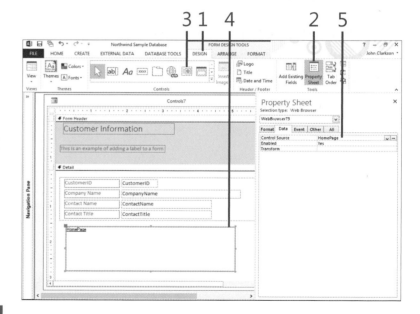

TIP If you add a text box to your form named txtURL and then set the web browser control's Control Source property to =txtURL, you can type a URL into the text box and have the results automatically displayed in the web browser control.

Working with tab controls

A tab control allows you to provide a control with multiple tab pages. You can give each tab page a name, and in design view, you can drag multiple controls from the Field List pane onto each tab page. This is very useful when you have a large number of controls that can be logically grouped together to provide a simpler interface consisting of multiple tab pages.

You can also use the dragging technique described in "Adding a subform to an existing form," on page 150, to drag subforms onto separate tab pages. This allows you to create very sophisticated interfaces with the tab control.

Work with a tab control

1   On the Form Design Tools ribbon, click the Design tab.

2   In the Tools section, click Add Existing Fields.

3   Click the tab control button in the Controls toolbox.

4   Position and resize the tab control.

(continued on next page)

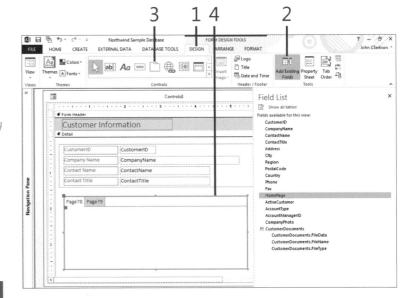

> **✓ TIP**   If you right-click with the tab control or a tab page selected, you will see options to insert or delete pages and change the page order. If you display the controls properties, the Caption property for each page allows the text in the tab to be changed. (If you don't type a caption, the tab name is used as the caption instead.)

Work with a tab control *(continued)*

5 Click the Page name (in this example, Page 78) to select a page in the tab control. (This highlights the tab page and not the tab control.)

6 Select one or more fields (hold down the Ctrl key for multiple selections).

7 Drag the fields onto the tab page.

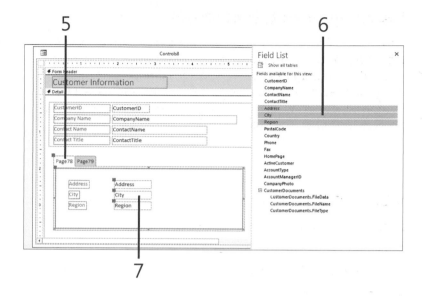

Creating command buttons

Command buttons perform a wide variety of actions. The Command Button Wizard provides a simple interface through which you can tailor the action of the button. When you create a command button with the Command Button Wizard, it will create a macro (the On Click embedded macro). We discuss macro programming is in Section 12, "Introducing the power of macros," starting on page 219.

For example, in the Form Operations category, the Open Form action displays a list of forms in your database and allows you to create a button that opens a form, and in the Report Operations category, the Preview Report action opens a selected report in print preview.

Create a command button

1 On the Form Design Tools ribbon, click the Design tab with a form open in design view.

2 Click the Command Button button in the Controls toolbox.

3 Position the button on the form.

4 Select a category of commands.

5 Select an action for the command category.

6 Click Next.

7 Select an image for the command button. (You can also browse to add your own images for the command buttons.)

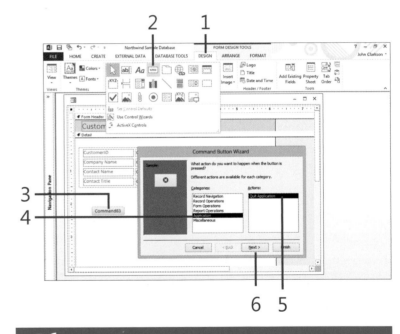

> ✓ **TIP** If you display the properties for this control and look on the Event tab, you will see that an embedded macro has been created for the On Click event. Clicking the build button (...) will then open the Macro Editing Tool, which allows you to create a rich and sophisticated sequence of steps behind the button click.

Setting control defaults

If you want the presentation of all your text boxes, combo boxes, or other controls on a form to be displayed using a particular choice of colors or fonts, you can change the default settings of each type of control on a form or report so that any new controls added to the form are displayed with these default settings. (Changing these settings does not affect existing controls on the form.)

In this example, we change the font size for the displayed text box and then, when a new text box is added to the form, it is displayed using the new control default.

Set control defaults

1 With a form in design view, select a label.

2 On the Form Design Tools Format tab, change the background color for the control.

3 On the Design tab, click the Controls toolbox drop-down arrow, and then click Set Control Defaults.

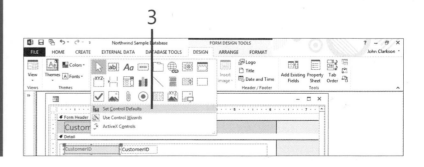

> **TIP** Each control has a set of presentation defaults. If you set up a form or report that has one of each desired control type with modified defaults (normally a label, text box, combo box, and list box, and background colors for the form sections are sufficient), on the Access Options popup window (which you access by clicking File on the Object Designers tab and choosing Options from the submenu), you can specify this name as the Form template or Report template. The presentation defaults are then used as a set of defaults when you create a new form or report. These settings will not be used by any of the wizards nor will they affect existing forms, but this is a valuable technique for standardizing the fonts and colors on controls.

Applying Office themes

Office themes offer three buttons (Themes, Colors, and Fonts) you can use to adjust the presentation of your forms and reports. The advantage of this feature is that you can apply specialized changes to a single object or apply changes to all matching objects. This provides you with a very quick method for changing the overall look of your reports and forms.

In this example, we show only the simplest of methods for applying changes by using a theme, but the technique equally applies to using the color or font options. You can apply these changes with a form either in layout or design view, but here we use layout view because it is probably the more natural view in which to apply these changes.

Apply an Office theme

1 With a form open in layout view, click the Design tab.

2 Click Themes, and as you point to a selected theme, you will see the form or report presentation change that reflects the theme.

3 Right-click the required theme, and choose Apply Theme To All Matching Objects from the shortcut menu. This means that if you open another form, it will also be displayed with the new theme.

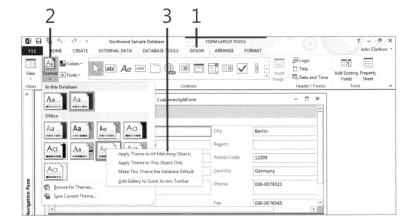

Preparing data to print using reports

10

Just as forms allow you to produce stunning on-screen presentations of data, reports offer a similar feature when you need to get a printed copy of the information. The main difference between a form and a report is that you can't edit data in a report, and you can't paginate and get a good paper layout with a form.

Access has powerful wizards to allow you to construct sophisticated presentations with reports. Like a form, a report can be based on a table or query, and it also supports layout and design views where you can add and change controls in a manner very similar to when you are working with a form.

Access reports also support multiple subreports, with as forms, as well as the use of macros and Visual Basic for Applications (VBA) to enhance your presentations. You should be careful to note the distinction between Print Preview and report view. Print Preview is designed to show the report layout before going to a printer, whereas report vew is for on-screen interaction with a report, making the report work more like a form.

In this section:

- Creating a tabular report with multiple tables
- Altering the presentation of controls
- Adding a running sum
- Managing data and page breaks
- Adding sorting and grouping on reports
- Avoiding blank pages
- Adding conditional formatting
- Creating a single record report with the Report Wizard
- Creating a parent/child report
- Using labels and managing columns and rows
- Working with layout view, report view, and Print Preview

Creating a tabular report with multiple tables

Like a form, a report can have a header and footer above and below the detail section, and within this it also supports a page header/footer. Reports are different from forms in that they allow the detail section to be surrounded by multiple groupings based on common field values. Each layer of grouping supports a group header for adding titles to columns and a group footer that can provide summary information for the group.

In this example, we show how to select fields from two related tables that will also introduce a single grouping for the data. The Report Wizard also prompts you to add extra levels of grouping.

Create a tabular report

1 Click the Create tab.

2 In the reports group, click Report Wizard.

3 In the Report Wizard, select your first table.

4 Choose fields from the first table.

5 On the same page, use the drop-down box to select a second, related table.

6 Choose fields from this second table.

7 Click Next.

(continued on the next page)

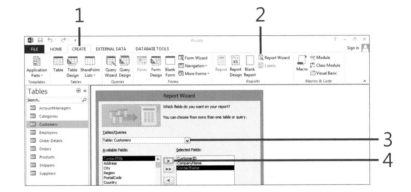

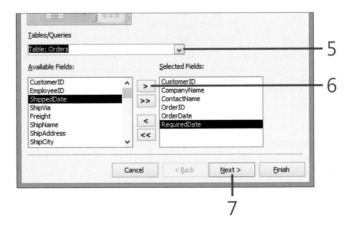

Create a tabular report *(continued)*

8 On the next page of the Report Wizard, you can choose how to view your data. In our example, we've chosen By Customers.

9 Click Next.

10 On the next page of the Report Wizard, select additional fields to group the data. Click Next.

(continued on the next page)

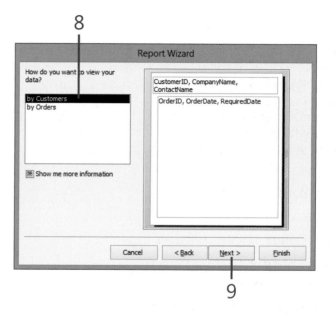

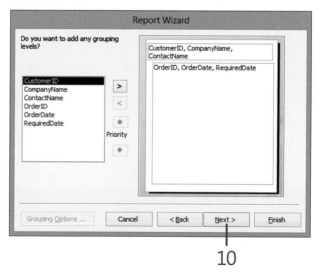

Create a tabular report   *(continued)*

11 On the next page of the Report Wizard, choose to sort by one or
more fields in the detail section.

12 Click Next.

13 On the next page of the Report Wizard, select the layout and orien-
tation for the report. Change the Layout option to Block.

14 Click Next.

(continued on the next page)

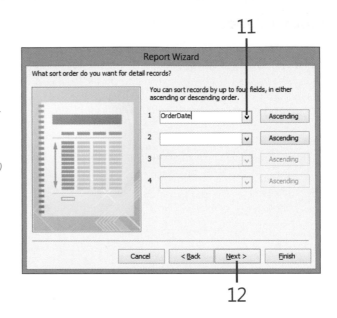

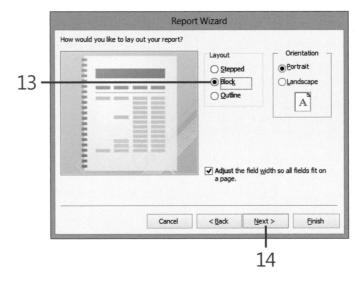

> **TIP**   If you create the report based on a single table or if you
> create a query involving a single table, the wizard will show
> different options for Layout (Columnar, Tabular, or Justified). Choose
> Tabular.

Create a tabular report *(continued)*

15 On the next page of the Report Wizard, optionally change the name of the report and then select whether to open the report in Print Preview or Design view. Click Finish. The completed report is now displayed in Print Preview.

16 On the Home tab, click View, and select Design View from the submenu.

17 For our example, in Design view you can see a new additional grouping on CustomerID added by the Report Wizard around the detail section. In this case, the grouping has a header but no footer. Adjust the width of any fields where the label or data is not fully visible.

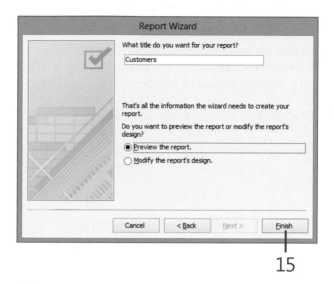

15

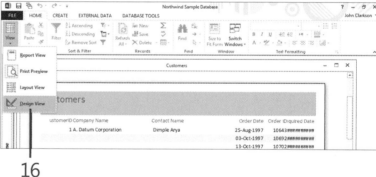

16

17

TIP When a number or date field does not have enough space to display the information, the data will be shown with pound or hash (#) symbols. In this situation, you need to alter the layout to resize the field to display the information.

Altering the presentation of controls on a page

In all these examples, we prepared our report using the Report Wizard, which means that the controls are not locked into a layout. We start by looking at how to perform basic adjustments to the presentation of controls on a report, such as altering a control width, or alignment, and splitting label text over multiple lines.

Unlike a form, which has a default view that you can set to Single Form or Continuous Form, a report always displays a continuous table of data. However, by moving controls and labels into the Detail section or group header/footer sections, we can change a tabulation to a single record style of presentation.

Alter the size and position of a control

1 Right-click the report in the navigation pane, and select Design View.

2 If you have a label that is too long and overlaps other labels, click into the text on a label in the page header and position the cursor where you want to split the label text over two lines.

3 Press Ctrl+Enter to split the title. (Shown here is the result of doing this on the Order Date label.) The page header's height will increase to accommodate the label over two lines.

(continued on the next page)

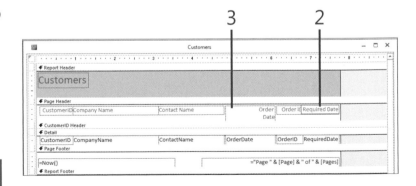

 TIP   If you already have a report open, use the View button on the Home tab to switch to Design view.

Alter the size and position of a control (continued)

4 To move a label and the control in the detail section together, click to select a label.

5 Hold down the Ctrl key, and select the corresponding field in the detail section. Use the mouse to drag both the label and field to a new position.

6 If you have a control and label that are not aligned, click to select a label.

7 Click to select the control in the detail section, holding down the Ctrl key so that both the label and the other control are selected.

8 Click the Arrange tab in the Report Design Tools tab.

9 Click Align in the Sizing & Ordering group.

10 On the drop-down menu, click Left to left-align the controls.

11 To make a label and control width the same, click Size/Space in the Sizing & Ordering group.

12 On the drop-down menu, select To Widest, which will change both controls to the largest width.

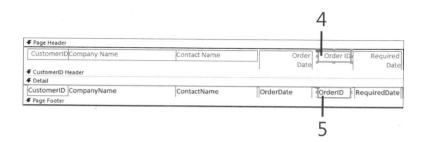

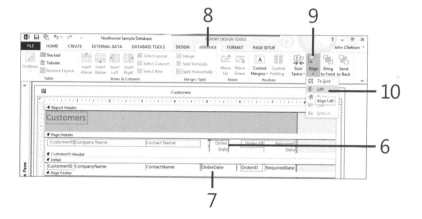

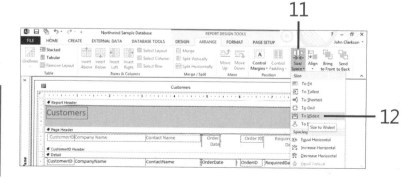

TIP To get fine control over moving a label, you can use the arrow keys to move the label and control. Holding down the Ctrl key while pressing the arrow keys will move the controls in smaller increments, and holding down the Shift key while pressing the arrow keys will resize the controls.

Working with controls and sections

One main differences between reports and forms is that reports have more sections, and by using grouping, further sections can be added to the report. You will often need to increase or decrease the available space in a section and move controls and labels between sections.

When moving controls from a detail section into a group header, you can produce a presentation that combines the tabulation of the detail section with a single record presentation in the header.

Move controls between sections

1   With your report in Design view, drag down any closed group header section to make space for moving controls.

2   We now want to reposition all labels inside the CustomerID group header so that they are repeated for each customer record. Drag the labels from the page header section into the group header. Some labels can be moved individually, and others can be moved with multiple labels selected.

(continued on the next page)

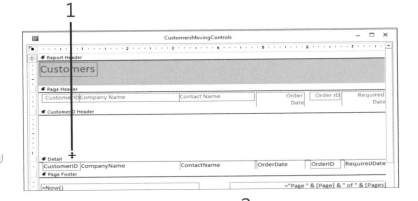

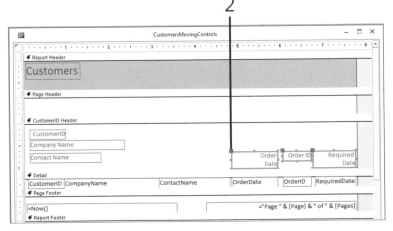

> ✓ **TIP**   Sometimes you might want to show a grouping field in the detail section while suppressing the display of duplicate values, or you might have other fields in the report where duplicate values need to be suppressed. Each control has a *Hide Duplicates* property to support this.

Move controls between sections (continued)

3 Move the controls that are common to the grouping field from the detail section into the group header. In our example, these are all the customer-specific fields. The group header now contains the parent fields, and the detail section contains the child fields.

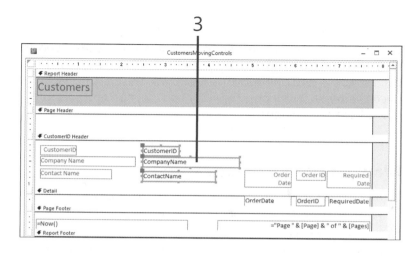

TIP When you move a label from a page header and its associated control has been moved from another section, notice that the label and control do not move together. You can attach the label to the control by cutting the label (press Ctrl+X) and pasting it onto the selected control. Also, to move the label to one section and the control to another section, cut the label and paste it into a different report section.

Using the *Can Grow* and *Can Shrink* Properties

The *Section* properties are related to controls, which also have *Can Grow* and *Can Shrink* properties that allow them to expand or contract to display a larger area of data. This means that you can manage the available spaces for each section and control.

You can see how information for the company name and other columns can be truncated, which you can alter to grow and display the truncated data.

Allow a section and controls to grow and shrink

1 In Design view, select the Detail section.

2 In the Tools group on the Design tab, click Property Sheet.

3 Click the Format tab.

4 Set the Can Grow property to Yes, and set the Can Shrink property to Yes.

5 Use the Ctrl key to select multiple controls.

6 Change the Can Grow property to Yes, and set the Can Shrink property to Yes.

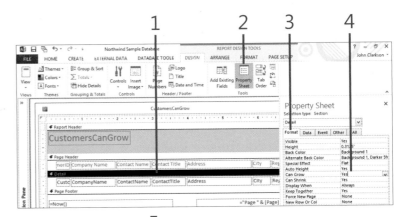

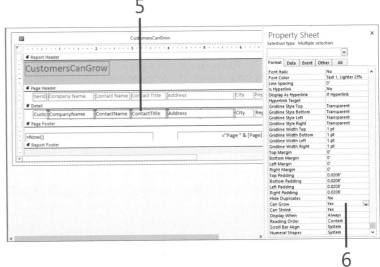

> ✓ **TIP** A fantastic feature in Access is that it allows you to change common properties for multiple controls at the same time. As you select multiple controls, the available properties will sometimes be reduced to only those properties common to the selected controls.

> ✓ **TIP** The *Section* properties are related to controls, which both have *Can Grow* and *Can Shrink* properties to allow them to expand or contract to display a larger area of data. This means that you can manage the available space for the controls and each section.

Adding a running sum

Text box controls have a *Running Sum* property, which, when set to true, causes the control to display a running total of a numerical field. You can set the Running Sum property either to ignore any groups and run over all data in the report or to run over a group, where it runs over only a single group value and is reset before producing results for the next group.

In our example, we apply the Running Sum property to the quantity for a sales order, and we set the running total to be over a grouping on the OrderID.

Add a running sum

1 In Design view, click a field that contains numerical data.

2 In the Tools group on the Design tab, click Property Sheet.

3 Click the Data tab.

4 Change the Running Sum property to Over Group.

TIP When adding a running sum or any summary calculation, you might want to display this at the bottom of each page. If you try to place a bound control in the page footer, you will see an error message displayed. To add these or similar calculation to a page footer, you must add an unbound control in the footer and then add program code to the report section. You might find it simpler to display the control in a group footer.

Managing data and page breaks

It is often very important to manage page breaks in your data. In this section, we look at two techniques for managing this. The first technique involves setting the *Force New Page* property (available on all sections except for the page header/footer). The second technique uses a property of all sections of a report (except the page header/footer) *Keep Together*. When this property is set to Yes, the report will throw a new page if it cannot fit all information within the section on the current page. By default, this property is set to true.

You should also look very carefully at the Keep Together property described in the next task, "Adding sorting and grouping on reports ," on page 188, because these topics are interrelated.

Force a new page

1   In Design view, select a group footer section.

2   In the Tools group on the Design tab, click Property Sheet.

3   Click the Format tab.

4   Set the Force New Page property to After Section.

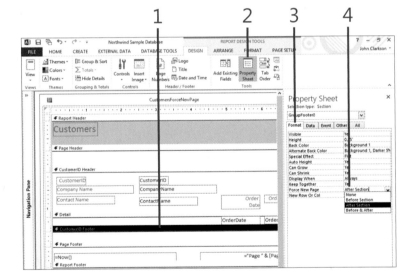

> **TIP**   In Design view (on the Design tab in the Controls group), clicking the Controls icon displays a Page Break control; this gives you finer control of where page breaks occur in a report.

Keep results together on the same page

1 In Design view, click Group & Sort in the Grouping & Totals group on the Design tab.

2 In the Group, Sort, And Total section, click More.

3 Select the option to keep the whole group together on one page.

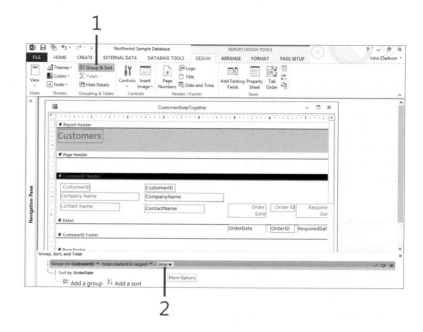

> ⚠️ **CAUTION** The Keep Together property keeps together only the information being displayed in the section to which it applies for each record. Groups have their own properties, which you can set to keep a group header, footer, and its detail section displayed on the same page.

Adding sorting and grouping on reports

Sorting and grouping provides a flexible way to add new sections around the detail section to organize your records. Each sort or group can have a header and/or footer area. The header displays titles and columns that are common to the records that will be displayed inside the group, and the footer displays summary information such as a record count or the sum of a particular value.

Adding grouping to your reports allows you create a parent/child-styled presentation of data without the need to use a subreport. In this case, you group on a parent field and move controls into the group header/footer.

Add a sort and group

1 In the Grouping & Totals group on the Design tab, with a report in Design view, click Group & Sort.

2 In the Group, Sort, And Total section, click Add A Group.

3 Select a field for the group.

4 In the Group, Sort, And Total section, click More.

5 Click the With No Totals drop-down list.

6 Select the primary key field.

7 In the Type field, select Count Records.

8 Select the Show Grand Total check box.

9 Select the Show Subtotal In Group Footer check box.

(continued on the next page)

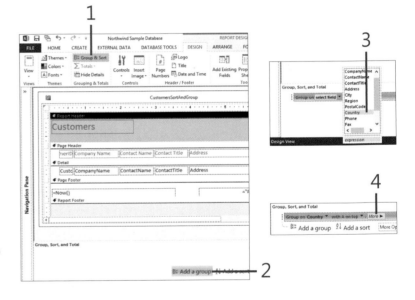

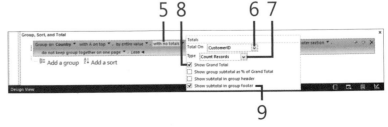

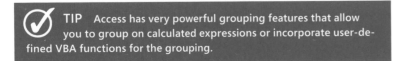

TIP Access has very powerful grouping features that allow you to group on calculated expressions or incorporate user-defined VBA functions for the grouping.

Add a sort and group *(continued)*

10 Select Keep Whole Group Together On One Page. Your report will now include the new grouping around the detail section.

11 On the Design tab, in the Tools group, click the Add Existing Fields icon.

12 Click the Country field.

13 Drag the Country field into the group header.

14 Drag the titles from the Page Header section into the group header.

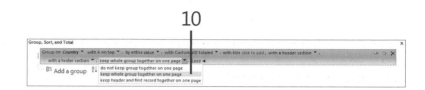

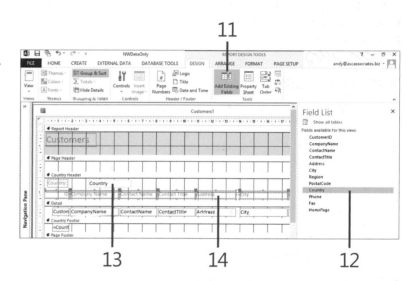

> ✓ **TIP** A fantastic feature in Access is that it allows you to change common properties for multiple controls at the same time. As you select multiple controls, the available properties will sometimes be reduced to only those properties common to the selected controls.

Avoiding blank pages

When you are formatting a report, if the width of the page allowing for margins exceeds the available paper width, the report will spill over onto additional pages. Sometimes this can display more data, and on other occasions, it displays alternating blank pages.

Because a report is set up with a particular printer installed on a system, when the report is used on a system with an alternative printer that supports different margins, you can find that a working report on one system produces blank pages on another system and therefore needs adjustment.

Remove a blank page

1 With a report opened in Design view, switch to Print Preview to see the formatting problem, and then Close Print Preview to return to Design view.

2 In Design view, click the Page Setup tab.

3 Click Page Setup in the Page Layout group.

4 Reduce the margin width, and click OK.

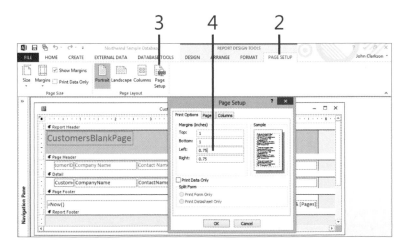

> **TIP** Other points to consider when removing blank pages include switching from portrait to landscape orientation, shrinking control widths, setting the control and section Can Grow properties to Yes, or moving labels and controls together in a section to provide a columnar layout, making the section narrower and taller.

Adding conditional formatting

Conditional formatting applies to both forms and reports and allows you to create colorful presentations in which you format a cell in a record to highlight its value as compared to other fields or values. A simple example would be to display all cell values of less than zero on a red background.

In addition to changing the formatting colors of a cell, you can display a data bar that shows the value compared to the field's range of values in the report or against a specific range of values, providing a quick visual indication of how the data compares against other values.

Add conditional formatting

1 Select a field that contains numerical values.

2 Click Conditional Formatting in the Control Formatting group on the Format tab.

3 Click New Rule.

4 Change the rule type to Compare To Other Records.

5 In the Type field, change Lowest to Number and Highest to Number. (The default compares against the lowest and highest values in the report.)

6 Type Values for the shortest and longest bars. In our example, we entered 100 to 1000.

7 Click OK. (Also click OK to close the Conditional Formatting Rules Manager dialog box, and select Layout View from the View drop-down menu on the Design tab.)

8 In layout view, click Conditional Formatting to make further changes to the presentation.

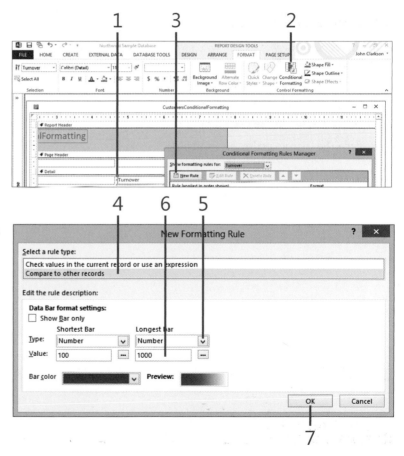

Creating a single record report with the Report Wizard

In a single record report, the field labels and controls are displayed in the Detail section; this is different from a tabular presentation because the controls and labels are attached and move together in the Detail section. In a tabular report, the labels are displayed in a section header and the controls are displayed in the Detail section, and they do not move together unless the report was created via the Report icon, which adds layouts to the controls.

If you create a report either by selecting from multiple tables in the Report Wizard or by using a query containing multiple tables, the Report Wizard does not display a columnar option to lay out the record but displays only tabular layout options.

Create a single record report

1 Click the Create tab.

2 Click Report Wizard in the Reports group.

3 Select a single table.

4 Select several fields from the table.

5 Click Next.

6 Do not select any fields for grouping. Click Next.

(continued on the next page)

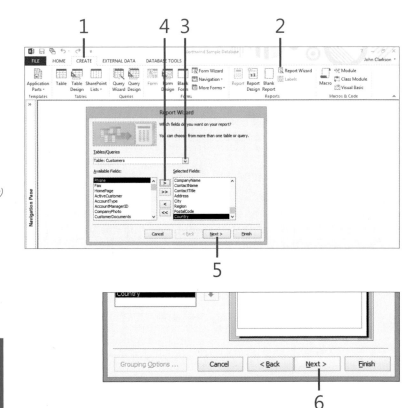

✓ TIP Do not add any grouping options in the Report Wizard. Otherwise, you will not be able to select a columnar report. You can add groupings to the report after you have finished using the Report Wizard.

Create a single record report

7 Select any fields for sorting the records.

8 Click Next.

9 Choose Columnar for the report layout.

10 Click Next. On the final page of the Wizard enter a name for the report and click Finish.

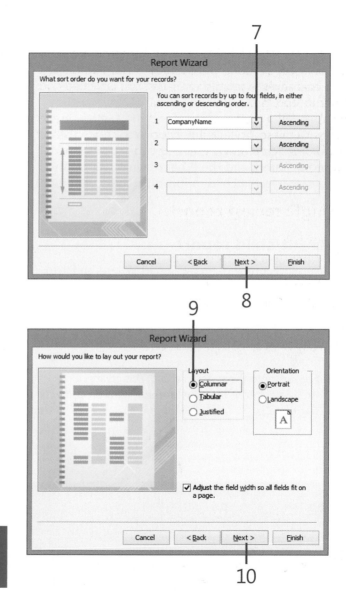

Creating a parent/child report

A parent/child report is similar to a parent/child form, where one table or query provides the parent record and another table or query contains the related child records, which are displayed in a subreport.

The Report Wizard does not have any options to create these parent/child reports. You start by creating two reports, one of which will be the parent and the other of which will be the child. Then you can drag the child report onto the parent report (while it is in Design view).

As an example, we will use a tabular list of orders, which we can create by using the Report Wizard. The table on which this report is created contains a linking field, which is the CustomerID, although the field does not need to be displayed on the report.

Our parent report will be a columnar report that we create by using the Report Wizard and which displays customer details. We will start with that report in Design view. The primary key on the parent is CustomerID, which will be used to link the parent report to the child subreport.

Create a parent/child report

1 Create a tabular subreport by using the Report Wizard, and then save and close the report.

2 With the parent report open in Design view (we have moved several fields to provide space for the subreport), position the report next to the navigation pane and select the child report to be positioned on the parent report.

3 Drag the child report onto the parent report. This creates a subreport control. Select Print Preview from the View drop-down menu on the Design tab.

(continued on the next page)

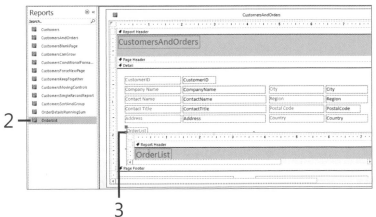

> **TIP** If you are having problems with the data in a subreport not being filtered by the parent record, display the Report Properties pane and examine the values in the *Link Master Fields* (parent) and *Link Child Fields* properties. These properties also have build buttons that can assist you in selecting the fields to use when linking the parent report to the child report.

Create a parent/child report

4 To see how the report would require further adjustment to prevent the split over two pages, click Two Pages on the Print Preview tab. In this example, the subreport control width needs to be reduced.

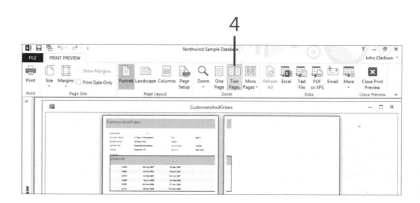

✓ **TIP** The child report contains a large report header (OrderList), which can be removed from the child report. Also, the heading titles for the child report are not displayed. To display these titles, you need to add a suitable grouping header on the child report and then move the column titles Order ID, Order Date, and Required Date from the page header into the group header in the subreport.

Using labels and managing columns and rows

Reports support portrait or landscape layouts, and in both cases you can alter the presentation to include Columns. With the columns presentation (which is used for labels and can also be used to present a directory-style layout of your data), the layout of records is split into several columns. The report can either show data in each column—filling the page for the first column and then moving to the next column—or display the data by filling all columns from left to right, working down each row in the page.

The Label Wizard is the easiest way to generate a set of labels, which you can then further adapt, although you can add this feature to any existing report.

Add a columns presentation

1 Select a table or query in the navigation pane.

2 Click the Create tab.

3 In the Reports group, click Labels.

4 Select an appropriate label.

5 Click Next, and on the next wizard page where you can change the fonts, click Next.

(continued on the next page)

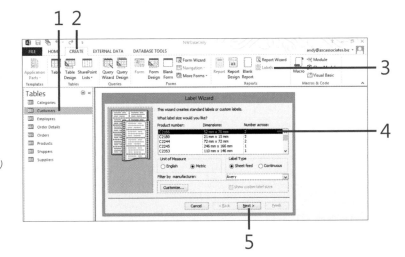

Add a columns presentation *(continued)*

6 Click a label field.

7 Add the field to the label expression, and repeat to build up a list of fields in the label.

8 Click Next. The next wizard screen allows you to choose fields for sorting. Make any appropriate choices, and click Next.

9 Add a suitable title the report.

10 Click Finish.

11 In the Page Layout group, you can click Columns to make further changes to the label layout. This will display the Page Setup popup window with the Columns tab selected.

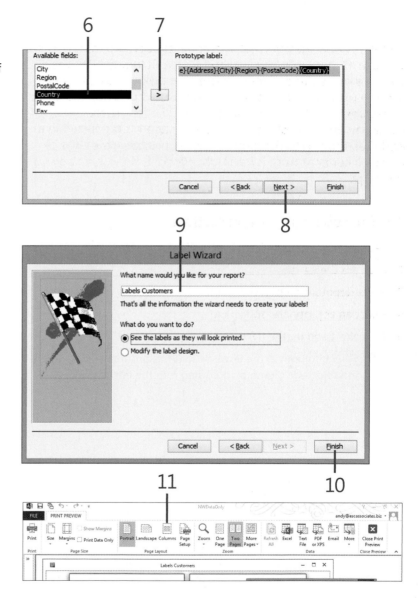

Working with layout view, report view, and Print Preview

When you double-click a report in the navigation pane, it opens the report in report view, which displays all the records as a continuous list. You can then switch the report into Print Preview to see the report paginated as it would be printed.

You can create forms and reports with controls organized in a layout. The layout presentation feature has the advantage of allowing you to easily modify the report while viewing data in layout view. Clicking the Report button on the Create tab will create a tabular report where the controls are placed in a layout. The options on the Arrange tab are intended for use with a layout presentation.

Alter a report in layout view

1 Select a table in the navigation pane.

2 Click the Create tab.

3 Click Report in the Reports group.

4 Click in a column row or heading.

5 Click the Arrange tab.

6 Click Select Column in the Rows & Columns group. You can reposition, the selected column by dragging it to the left or right.

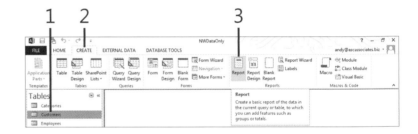

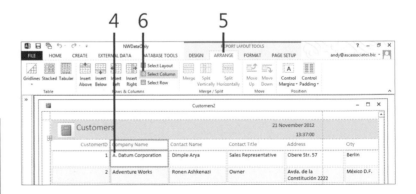

> **TIP** You might find that it is easier to alter your presentation by removing any control layouts. However, if you do this, you will lose many of the benefits associated with working in layout view. By working with control layouts, using the icons in the Rows & Columns group on the Arrange tab, you'll find that altering the layout is greatly simplified.

Switch between report view and Print Preview

1 Double-click a report to open it in report view.

2 Click the View drop-down arrow, and select Print Preview.

Exchanging data

11

Access has fantastic support for getting data into and out of your database by using import and export procedures. You can import data into existing tables, or create new tables as the data is imported. In this section, we demonstrate the most popular formats for exchanging data.

In addition to importing and exporting, you can link to the data. This provides a dynamic link so that you will always see the latest data in the other data source, and when linked to data in another Access database or Excel spreadsheet, it will also dynamically reflect any changes made to the data structures in those files.

If you have data in databases such as IBM, Oracle, Informix, SharePoint, or SQL Server, you will find that Access also supports methods to exchange data by linking or importing from those sources via ODBC (Open Database Connectivity), which is a standard method for interconnecting systems.

In this section:

- Importing data and objects from Access
- Linking to data in Access
- Importing data from Excel
- Linking to data in Excel
- Importing data from text files using specifications
- Exporting data to Excel
- Refreshing linked tables when files are changed
- Working with saved imports and exports
- Exporting data as PDF documents

Importing data and objects from Access

When you import from another Access database, you can choose to import any combination of tables, queries, forms, reports, macros, or modules. For each type of object, you have the option to select all the objects or to select individual objects of each type.

When importing related tables, you import the relationships by default. Options are available to exclude relationships, to import only structures and not data, and to create new tables when importing data from queries rather than importing the query.

Import data and objects from an Access database

1 Click Access in the Import & Link group on the External Data tab.

2 Keep the default selection to import tables, queries, forms, reports, macros, and modules into the current database.

3 In the File Open popup window, browse to locate the database file. Select the file, and click Open.

4 Click OK.

(continued on the next page)

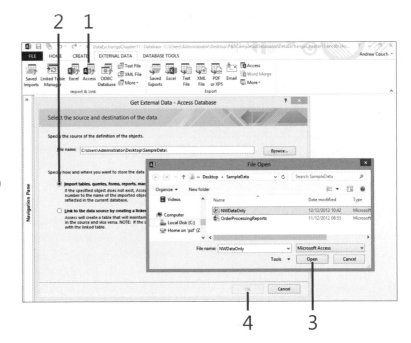

Import data and objects from an Access database *(continued)*

5 Use the tabs to display objects in the database to be imported.

6 Select objects to import from each tab.

7 Click Options to see more options when importing data.

8 Click OK.

9 If you will be repeating this operation later, select the Save Import Steps check box.

10 Click Save Import.

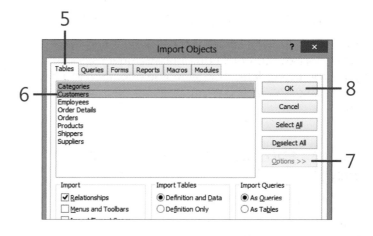

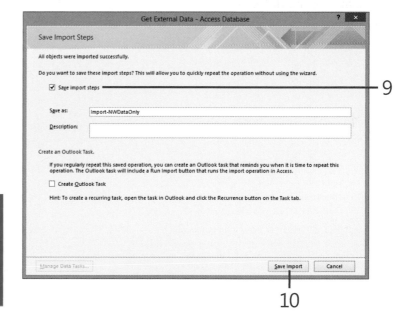

> **TIP** When you are importing an object and an existing object in the database has the same name, Access will rename the imported object, appending a number to the end of the name to resolve the conflict. For example, if you import a table called Products when you already have a table with that name, the new table will be called Products1.

Linking to data in Access

Rather than importing data from an Access database, you can create links to the tables in an other database. You will then be connected to the live data in the other database, and this will save you from needing to regularly import data from the other system.

In addition to not having to copy data, if the linked tables, design is changed in the database to which you are linked, you will automatically see those design changes when next opening the linked table in your database. (If your linked table is open, you will need to close it before making any design changes in the database to the table to which you are linked.)

Link to data in an Access database

1 Click Access in the Import & Link group on the External Data tab.

2 Select Link To The Data Source By Creating A Linked Table.

3 Browse to locate the database file. Select the file and click Open.

4 Click OK.

(continued on the next page)

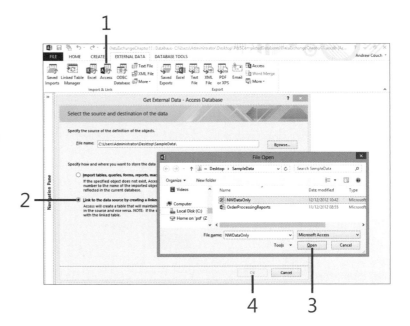

Link to data in an Access database *(continued)*

5 Select the tables to be linked.

6 Click OK.

7 A linked table is shown with a different icon in the navigation pane.

> ✓ **TIP** Access databases are often designed where all the items except the Tables are held in one database, and the Tables are held in a different database. This method enables users to have their own copy of the application on their local machine, but link to and share the data from another Access database on the network.

Importing data from Excel

When importing data from Excel, if you have only one worksheet and no named ranges defined, the wizard does not prompt you to make any additional decisions (as described shortly in step 5). But if you have either multiple worksheets or one or more ranges defined in a single worksheet or in multiple worksheets, you are prompted to select either a worksheet or a named range.

When importing data, you will also find that Access makes a best assessment of the appropriate data type to use for each column, but you can review and change the choice of data type before importing the data.

Import data from Excel

1 Click Excel in the Import & Link group on the External Data tab.

2 Keep the default selection to import the source data into a new table in the current database.

3 Browse to locate the Excel file. Select the file and click Open.

4 Click OK.

5 Select the required worksheet from which to import the data, and click Next.

(continued on the next page)

TIP The wizard also offers an option to directly append data into an existing table. However, it is often better to import data into a temporary staging table and then use the techniques described in Section 7, "Modifying data using queries," starting on page 117, using action queries to transfer the data into your main tables after checking the data.

Import data from Excel *(continued)*

6 If your spreadsheet includes column headings, select the First Row Contains Column Headings check box, and click Next.

7 To change imported data types for a column, select the column. Use the horizontal scroll bar to see more columns from the source data.

8 Select a data type in the Data Type drop-down box and click Next.

9 Allow Access to add a primary key, or choose a column to use as the primary key. Click Next.

10 Type a name for the imported data table and click Finish.

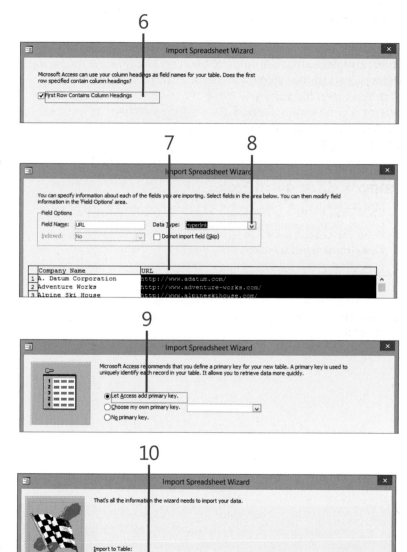

TIP After you complete the import steps you will be prompted with a screen to save the imported steps. This option allows you to repeat the the saved operation, as described later in this section.

Linking to data in Excel

The ability to link Access to data in Excel can mean that rather than repeatedly importing data, you can link directly to the data in the spreadsheet. This means that you will always be working with the latest dataset.

If you link to an Excel Worksheet and columns are subsequently altered in the spreadsheet, when you reopen the table you will see the linked data reflecting any structural changes to the spreadsheet. If you would prefer not to see these changes, you could link to a named range of cells in a worksheet instead.

Link to data in Excel

1 Click Excel in the Import & Link group on the External Data tab.

2 Select Link To The Data Source By Creating a Linked Table.

3 Browse to locate the Excel file. Select the file and click Open.

4 Click OK. You will be asked the same series of questions as described in the preceding task, "Import data from Excel" on page 206 (steps 5 to 10).

5 The linked table is shown with a different icon in the navigation pane.

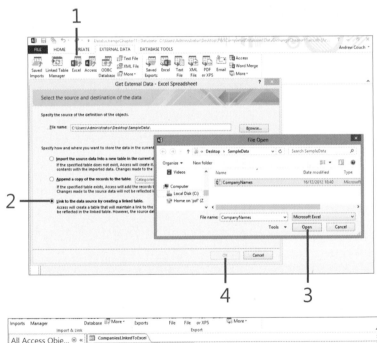

TIP When you link to an Access table, the linked table will allow you to edit and insert data, but when you are linked to an Excel spreadsheet, you will find that the Access application cannot modify the data because you have a read-only link to the Excel data.

Refreshing linked tables when files are changed

If you have linked tables to Access or Excel and if the files to which you are linking are moved to a different folder or the file name is changed, the links will no longer work. The Linked Table Manager allows you to select several linked tables and then inform Access of the new file path/name to the linked file.

If you know that a file name/path has changed, when relinking you should select the option Always Prompt For A New Location. If that option is not selected, when you refresh the links you will be prompted to specify a valid file path each time a link cannot be refreshed.

Refresh linked tables

1 Click Linked Table Manager in the Import & Link group on the External Data tab.

2 Click to select any links that need to be refreshed.

3 Select the Always Prompt For New Location check box.

4 Click OK.

5 Locate the file at the new location, and click Open.

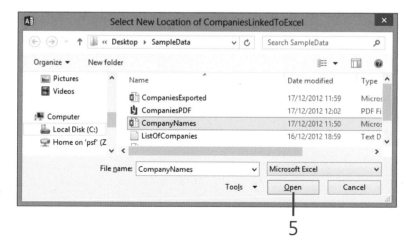

> ✓ **TIP** For links to Access and Excel worksheets, if the source data structure changes, the links do not need to be manually refreshed; they automatically display the latest structure. But if the links connect to tables in SQL Server or another database server, when the table structures change in the other database you will need to refresh those links.

Importing data from text files using specifications

The Import Text Wizard is a very sophisticated tool that allows you to import data in a wide variety of formats. The most popular text format is called *delimited*. In this format, columns are separated by a comma and text fields are surrounded with double quotes. You might occasionally come across a file that uses different delimiters, and the wizard can accommodate this.

The second format you might come across is fixed width, where every field has a fixed number of characters. The wizard will also help you to decide on column boundaries when you are working with this format.

Import data from a text file

1 Click Text File in the Import & Link group on the External Data tab.

2 Keep the default selection to import the source data into a new table in the current database.

3 Browse to locate the text file. Select the file and click Open.

4 Click OK.

(continued on the next page)

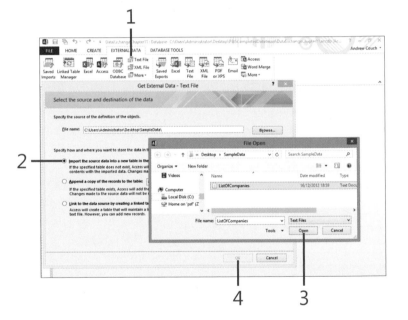

Import data from a text file *(continued)*

5 Select either Delimited or Fixed Width, according to the text file format. Delimited is the more common choice. If you want to see more advanced features of the Import Text Wizard, continue with step 6; otherwise, click Next and proceed to step 10.

6 Click Advanced.

7 Adjust any of the advanced settings associated with the text import.

8 Click Save As to save your settings as a specification.

9 Type a name for the specification, and click OK. Click OK to close the Advanced screen.

(continued on the next page)

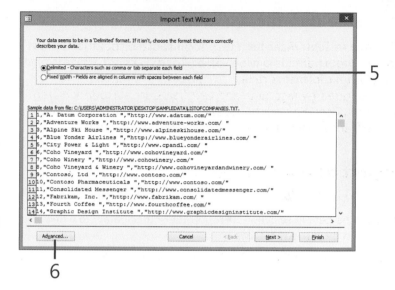

5

6

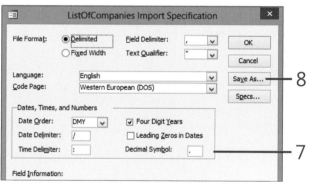

8

7

9

TIP Import specifications allow you to set up specialized settings for controlling how a file is imported. You can then reload them when repeating an import process. Usually, you will not need this extra flexibility, but if required, it can prove very useful.

Import data from a text file *(continued)*

10 If your first row in the text file contains field names, select the First Row Contains Field Names check box, and click Next. (Our example does not contain this row.)

11 To change imported data types for a column, select the column.

12 Select a data type in the Data Type drop-down box. Use the horizontal scroll bar to view the other columns from the data source.

13 Click Next.

(continued on the next page)

10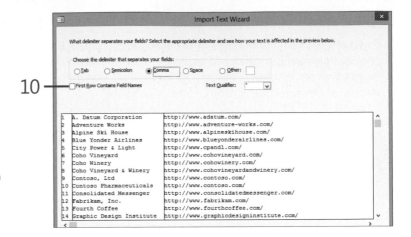

11 12

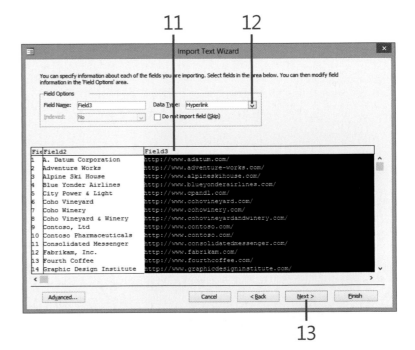

13

Import data from a text file (continued)

14 Allow Access to add a primary key, or choose a column to use as the primary key. Click Next.

15 Type a name for the imported data table, and click Finish.

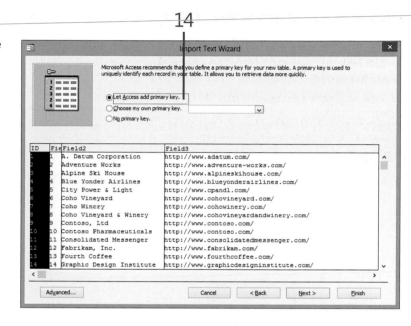

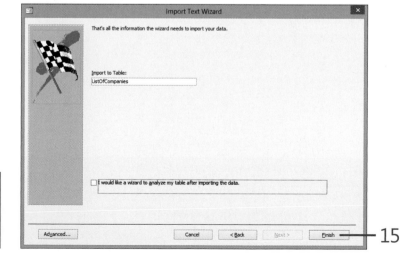

> **TIP** When importing data Access gives you three choices for setting the new primary key on a table. The simplest option is to accept the default choice and Let Access add primary key, this will add an autonumber field called ID to your table.

Exporting data to Excel

Access supports a wide range of formats for exporting data, and in this task, we demonstrate one of the most popular—Excel. After exporting data, you are prompted to save the export. Saving an export allows you to easily repeat it at a later date.

You can export data by using a table, query, form, or report.

Export data to Excel

1 In the navigation pane, highlight the object you want to export.

2 Click Excel in the Export group on the External Data tab.

3 Type a file name for the exported file.

4 Choose the file format.

5 Click OK.

(continued on the next page)

Using a query allows you to choose only the required subset of data, rather than including all the columns and rows in the underlying tables of data.

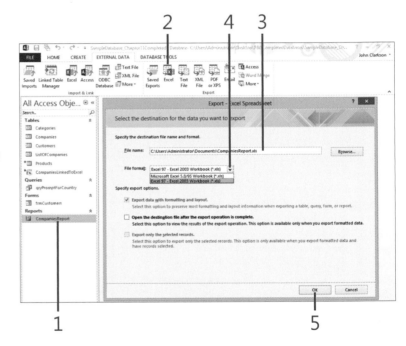

TIP In Section 6, "Selecting data using queries," starting on page 95 we explain how to create a query that prompts for filter criteria when opened. This type of parameterized query can be used when you are exporting data and provides a great way to add flexibility to your export routines.

Export data to Excel *(continued)*

6 If you will be repeating this operation later, select the Save Export Steps check box.

7 Click Save Export.

6

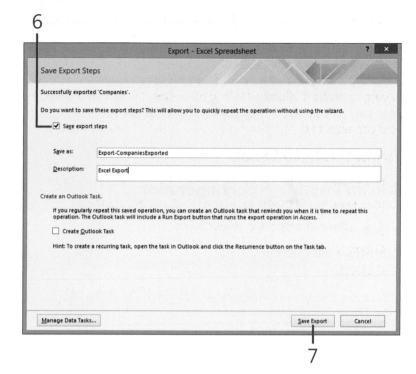

7

Working with saved imports and exports

Saving imports and exports allows you to repeatedly run data imports and exports with minimum effort. When you first import or export data, Access promptes you to save the import/export operation. If you save the operation at this time, you can later take advantage of this feature to rerun the process.

If the operation involved importing or exporting data and you have an existing file on your machine or a table in your database, you will be prompted to overwrite the object (except when importing from an Access database where, if the table exists, the new imported copy will be named with a suffix, such as Products1, Products2, and so on). If you select No, the operation will be canceled.

Run an import/export operation

1 Click Saved Imports in the Import & Link group on the External Data tab.

2 Select an import to run.

3 Click Run.

4 Click Yes to overwrite the table, or click No to cancel the import.

(continued on the next page)

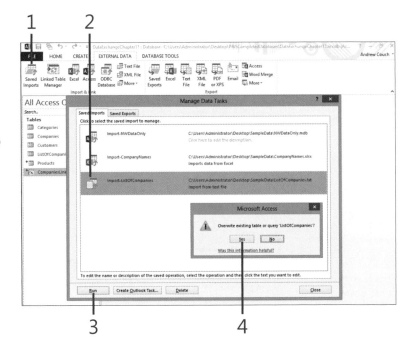

Run an import/export operation *(continued)*

5 Click the Saved Exports tab.

6 Select an export to run.

7 Click Run.

8 Click Yes to overwrite the file, or click No to cancel the export.

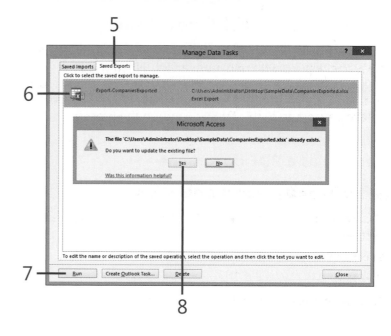

SEE ALSO In Section 12 "Introducing the power of macros" we will describe how macros can be used to repeat a saved import/ export.

Exporting data as PDF documents

A great feature in Access is the ability to easily facilitate exchanging information in the PDF file format. This allows you to export a complex report as a PDF file. Access also supports the alternative Microsoft standard XPS (XML Paper Specification).

Exporting data in PDF format is not limited to exporting a report. You can also export data in tables, queries, and forms in PDF format.

Save data as a PDF document

1 Select an object in the navigation pane.

2 Click PDF Or XPS in the Export group on the External Data tab.

3 Click Options to display other publishing options.

4 Click OK.

5 Click Publish to export the data.

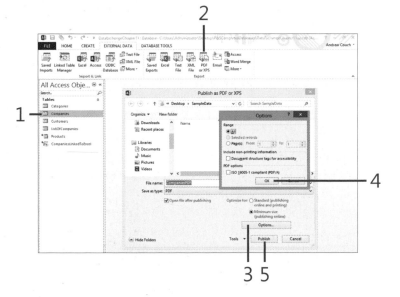

TIP If you have a report open in print preview, you can use the PDF or XPS icon on the print preview ribbon tab to publish the report.

Introducing the power of macros

12

Unlike Excel, which has a macro recording tool that creates code that you can then edit in the VBA editor, Access has two separate approaches to programming. The first is macro programming (there is no recording tool), which comes equipped with a special macro designer and set of macro commands. The second approach is VBA programming, which has an editor and environment very similar to the Excel programming environment. There is a crossover between the macro commands and VBA programming—that is, macros can be converted to VBA, and VBA can make use of macro commands.

Macros have many uses, including linking together user interface elements like forms, queries and reports, performing complex data validation, or executing sequences of operations to import and process sets of data.

In programming macros, you can save sequences of instructions either as a stand-alone macro, which you can execute from the navigation pane, or as an embedded macro inside a form/report.

In this section:

- Enabling macro commands and disabling Trusted Documents
- Linking together forms
- Linking a form to a query
- Validating data entered in controls
- Making controls change other controls
- Executing a saved import/export
- Processing data with action queries

Enabling macro commands and disabling Trusted Documents

Before you can use macro programming in your database, you need to enable macros in the Access installation. This process is described in "Change the default database options" on page 72). Refer to this task to make any further changes to settings described in this section.

After you enable macros, 20 macro commands will remain disabled and will not be visible in the macro designer. These commands can be made available only in Trusted Documents

or when the Trusted Documents feature is disabled. You should refer to your company's policy on Trusted Documents for advice on this. In this exercise, we demonstrate how to disable this feature and thus enable these additional commands.

Disable Trusted Documents

1 Enable macros as described in "Change the default database options" on page 72, then select Trusted Documents from the options on the left in the Trust Center window.

2 Select the Disable Trusted Documents check box, click OK to close any open windows, and then close and reopen your database.

(continued on the next page)

1

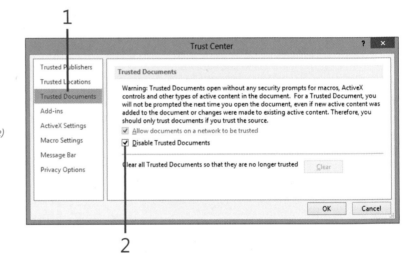

2

⚠ **CAUTION** The methods described in this book are intended to help you get started quickly and should not be interpreted as recommending a standard configuration for your Office software. For further details about Trusted Documents and other security issues, visit the Microsoft Trustworthy Computing page at *www.microsoft.com/about/twc/en/us/default.aspx?CE=Nav2b.*

Disable Trusted Documents *(continued)*

The macro commands listed in the following table operate only in Trusted Documents. You will find that the ImportExportData, SetValue, and SetWarnings commands are especially useful to have available when you are creating macros.

Macro commands

Data import/ export commands	Database objects	Filter/query/ search commands	Macro commands	System commands	User interface commands
ImportExportData	CopyObject	RunSQL	Echo	OpenSharePointList	ShowToolbar
ImportExportSpreadsheet	DeleteObject		OpenVisualBasicModule	OpenSharePoint RecycleBin	
ImportExportText	RenameObject			PrintOut	
ImportSharePointList	SaveObject			RunApplication	
RunSavedImportExport	SetValue			SendKeys	
				SetWarnings	

> ⊘ **TIP** If you do not trust the use of these commands in your database, you might get confused when, after searching online to find further examples, you fail to reproduce actions; as the commands are not be listed in the macro designers list of available actions.

Linking together forms

The OpenForm, OpenReport, OpenTable, and OpenQuery macro commands are among the most common and easiest to use. These commands allow you to open other forms, print reports, or display data in tables and queries. Normally, these macro commands are used on a command button control's OnClick event, but they can also be used as macros independent of a form.

Each control on a form has a set of events, and the On Click event for a button is activated when a user clicks the button. You will find that you do not need to understand all the available events and that you can accomplish most programming with only a few of them.

Create an embedded macro to open a form

1 With a form in Design view, click to expand the controls list, and turn off the Use Control Wizards option.

2 Click the Button control, and click in the form to add the button to the form.

3 In the Property Sheet pane, click the Event tab, then click the Build button for the On Click event.

4 In the Choose Builder dialog box, select the Macro Builder, and click OK.

5 In the Add New Action drop-down box, select OpenForm from the list of commands.

(continued on the next page)

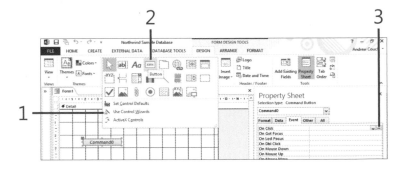

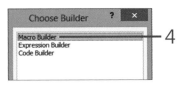

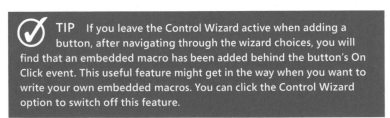

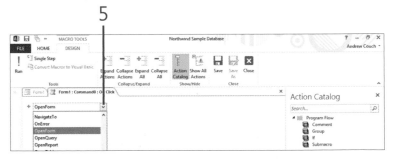

> ✓ **TIP** If you leave the Control Wizard active when adding a button, after navigating through the wizard choices, you will find that an embedded macro has been added behind the button's On Click event. This useful feature might get in the way when you want to write your own embedded macros. You can click the Control Wizard option to switch off this feature.

Create an embedded macro to open a form *(continued)*

6 Select another form to display by using the Form Name drop-down list of available forms.

7 Save and close the macro design tool. If you now display your form in Form view and click the command button, it will open the other form that you defined in the OpenForm macro command.

8 Return to Design view, and add a text box control to the form. Ensure that you change the control name. (In our example, it is called txtCountry.) Save your form.

9 Click to select the button control you added in step 2. Then click the Build button to return to the macro editor, and change the macro code embedded on your button.

10 Change the Where Condition so that data in the form that you open will be filtered by the data entered into the text box control. In our example, txtCountry is the control name, and the form we are opening is based on a table that has a field called [Country].

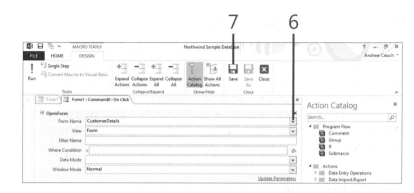

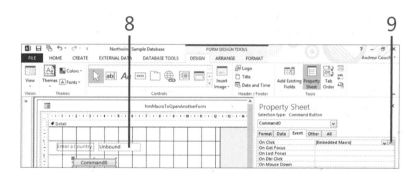

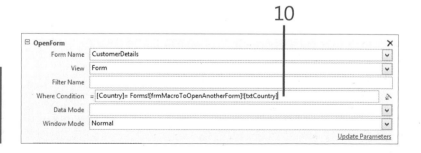

TIP As you start typing in the Where Condition box, IntelliSense will help you locate a form. After typing **Forms!**, you will see a list of available forms. Then, after you select a form and type the **!** character, a list of controls on the form is displayed.

Linking a form to a query

A popular design technique in creating a user interface is to use a method often called *query by form*. The idea is to create a query that has filter criteria that directly references one or more controls on a form. The user then types a value into the control on the form and clicks a button on the form, which opens either a query or a form/report based on a query, where the query links back to filter by the value entered on the form.

In our example, we will make the form open the query, but you could easily change this to open a form or report based on that query.

Link a form to a table or query

1 With a form in Design view, add a text box control. This text box will contain a value that will be used to filter data in a query.

2 Type a name for the text box control. (Naming controls will make creating expressions easier when you have several controls on a form.)

3 Save the form, but do not close it.

4 Create a query, and choose a field that will be filtered against the data in the control on the form we created.

5 Save the query.

6 Click in the Criteria row, in the column against which we'll be filtering the data.

7 Click Builder to open the Expression Builder popup window.

(continued on the next page)

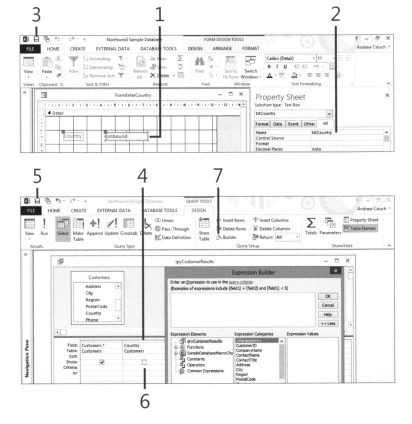

Link a form to a table or query *(continued)*

8 In the Expression Elements pane, browse the tree of information to locate the form that you created in earlier steps. (If you have many forms and you know that the form you are looking for is open, select Forms; then select Open Forms to display only a list of forms that are open. This is particularly useful when you are referencing controls on subforms.) Select the form.

9 Double-click the text control that we added to that form. Click OK.

10 Save and then close the query. Return to your form in Design view, and repeat steps 2–5 of the previous task ("Create an embedded macro to open a form" on page 222), where we added a command button to the form and displayed the macro design tool for the On Click event on the command button. However, this time choose the macro command OpenQuery in step 5.

11 From the available list of queries, select the query that you saved. Then save and close the macro window. You will now have a form with a control into which you can type a value and a button that opens a query that filters the data by the choice you have typed into the form.

8   9

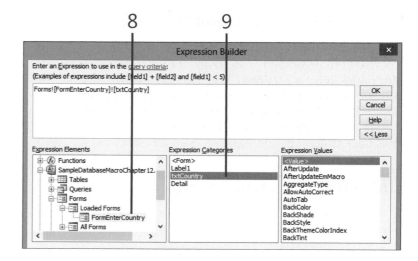

10

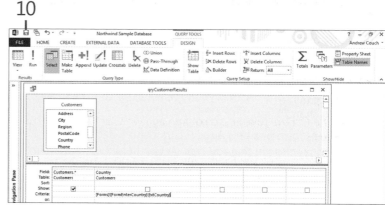

11

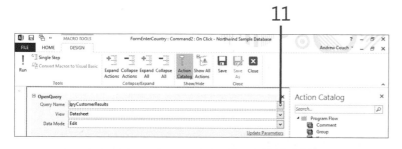

TIP You can enhance this method by adding a Requery macro command, which will update the query after you make a change in the text box on your form without the need to close the query window.

TIP The symbol ! is part of the syntax used to refer to objects inside a collection. Therefore, the syntax in this example translates to "look in the Forms collection for a form, and then look in that form's Controls collection for a control."

Validating data entered in controls

Controls on a form have a Before Update event that enables you to use macro commands to add actions when a user enters data before the entry is accepted. You can then decide whether to accept or reject the data entered in the control.

The Form's Before Update event executes before a record is saved. You can use this event to check the data, comparing values in multiple controls, before accepting or rejecting changes. If you need to cross-validate controls, it is often simpler to write the macro checking actions on the forms event, rather than repeating similar operations on several different controls.

Validate data entered in a control

1 In Design view, locate a control on which you want to add validation, and click the Event tab in the Property Sheet pane to display the event properties. In our example, we have created a new form and added an unbound text box control to the form.

2 Click the build button for the Before Update event, and select Macro Builder.

3 Select the If command in the Add New Action field. This is a conditional logic block where we can test a value and take an action.

4 Type the expression **NZ(txtLowerCount) < 10**; IntelliSense will display a list of controls after you type **NZ**. (Our control is called txtLowerCount.)

5 In the drop-down box below the If command, select the MessageBox action in the Add New Action field. Type a warning message and a title for the MessageBox action.

(continued on the next page)

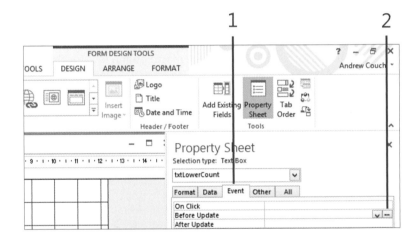

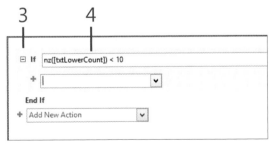

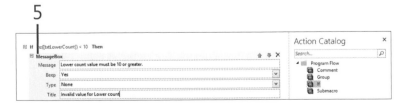

Validate data entered in a control *(continued)*

6 In the Add New Action field below the MessageBox action (but still inside the If block), select the command CancelEvent. This will reject the user's changes.

7 Save and close the macro designer. If you now view your form and type values in the field, you should find that the validation rule displays a message box and cancels your action when an invalid date has been entered.

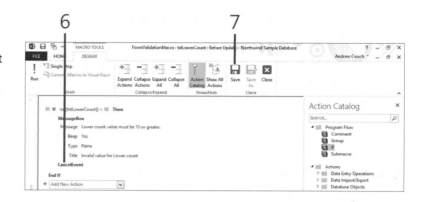

Making controls change other controls

Controls on a form have an After Update event that occurs after a successful Before Update event. If the Before Update event cancels the data change because it fails validation (as previously described), the After Update event will not fire. The After Update event is used to take action following a successful change to data, and one possible implementation is in changing how other controls can be used following a change in the data.

In addition to each control having an After Update event, the form also has an After Update event, after changes have been successfully validated for the record, which you can use to take further action based on values in several controls.

Change other controls

1 In Design view, locate a control to which you want to add an After Update action, and click the Event tab in the Property Sheet pane. In our example, we took the form from the previous task ("Validate data entered in a control" on page 226) and added an additional unbound text box (which has the Enabled property set to false).

2 Click the build button for the After Update event, and select Macro Builder.

(continued on the next page)

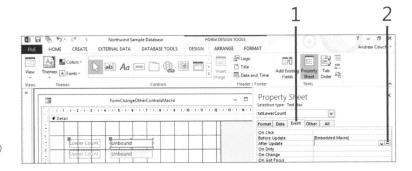

Making controls change other controls *(continued)*

3 On the Macro Tools Design tab, select Show All Actions. (Otherwise, you will not see the SetValue macro command in the drop-down list of commands.)

4 Add a SetProperty command. In our example, this will enable a second control when the first control has been validated and the After Update macro fires.

5 Add a SetValue macro command. In our example, we set the value of our second control to the same value entered in the first control. (IntelliSense will assist you when you are typing data in the Item and Expression fields.)

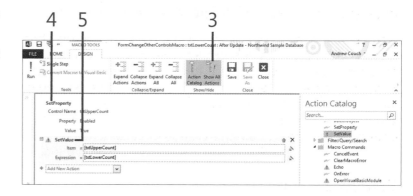

> ✓ **TIP** The Action Catalog on the right side of our screen provides an alternative method for both displaying the available macro commands and selecting a command. If you double-click a command, it will be added on the left. Also notice the warning triangle shown next to all commands that are available only in a Trusted Document.

Processing data with action queries

Section 7, "Modifying data using queries," starting on page 117, explains how action queries can update, insert, and delete data. When you need processing that executes a sequence of action queries, macros enable you to run those action queries to make bulk changes to the data in your system.

The OpenQuery macro will either open and display the results of a selected query or execute an action query with prompting for changing the data. By using the Set Warnings macro, you can switch off the prompting while the macro is executing.

In this example, we are going to use two action queries, first to empty a table and then to populate the table with data.

Empty and populate a table of data

1 Create an action query to delete all the data in a table that you regularly need to populate from another table of imported data.

2 Create an action query that will append a set of records from another table to the same table from which you deleted all the records. (We are going to assume here that you regularly import data from another system into a table and that you then need to further process that data into other tables in your database.)

(continued on the next page)

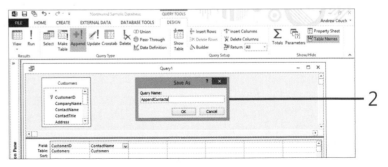

> ✓ **TIP** When you are developing a stand-alone macro, you can take advantage of the Run button on the far left of the ribbon to execute your macro while staying in the design tool. You can also click the Single Step button to allow execution of the macro one step at a time.

Empty and populate a table of data *(continued)*

3 Click the Create tab.

4 Click Macro.

5 Add an OpenQuery command.

6 Select the query that empties the data from your table.

7 Add an OpenQuery command.

8 Select the query that adds data to the empty table.

9 Save the macro.

10 Type a name for the macro, and click OK. At this point, you should save and test the macro.

11 Add the Set Warnings command, with Warnings On set to No. This prevents the prompting boxes from displaying when you are executing the query. (When you have verified that it executes correctly, you might want to switch off the built-in warnings when executing an action query.)

12 Add the Set Warnings command, with Warnings On set to Yes. It is very important that you always switch the standard warnings back on.

13 Add a MessageBox command to indicate that the processing is completed.

14 Use the up and down arrows to move your commands to the correct position in the macro sequence.

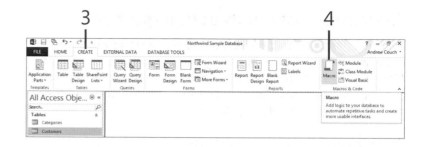

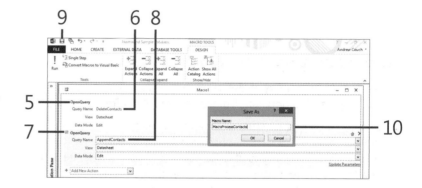

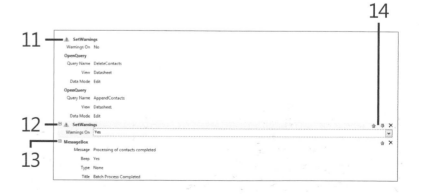

Executing a saved import/export

Macro commands are provided for running the saved import/export processes that we described in Section 11, "Exchanging data," starting on page 201. For example, on a form, these commands could allow you to create a button that executes a sequence of import/export processes to manage your data.

In this example we will show how to create a macro that is not embedded inside a form. You can then execute this macro from the navigation pane, or alternatively, you could use the RunMacro command inside an embedded macro on a button on a form. (Macros can run other macros.)

Execute a saved import/export

1 Click the Create tab.

2 Click Macro.

3 Click Show All Actions.

4 Select the RunSavedImportExport action. (You will need to have already saved an import/export to use this.) Select the file to import or export.

5 Click Save.

6 Type a name for the macro, and click OK. In the navigation pane, a new object type will be shown (unless you have previously created macros). Double-click the macro to execute the operation.

7 To edit your macro, display the macro in the navigation pane, right-click, and select Design View.

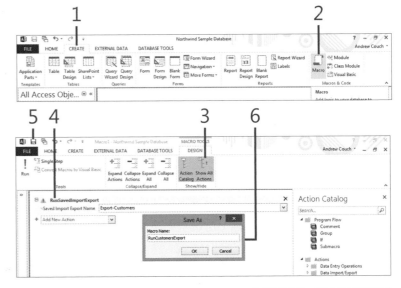

> ✓ **TIP** You will notice when executing this macro that there is not a message indicating that the macro has executed. As a final step, you could add a message box to indicate that the macro has completed the export.

Administrating a database

13

In this section, we will look at a number of Access features that will assist you in managing and configuring your database.

The Compact & Repair feature helps you optimize the database for best performance and resolve any inconsistencies.

In protecting your data, we look at how to password-protect and encrypt your database to prevent others from opening it either with Access or with another tool.

The Analysis Tools feature enables you to use the Database Documenter tool to produce printed documentation of your design. The Performance Analyzer database tool will give you advice and tips on improving your design, and you can use the Table Analyzer Wizard to restructure a table into a more consistent format for use in a relational database.

Inside Access is a map of how all your tables, queries, forms, and reports are dependent on each other. The Object Dependencies feature allows you to examine this map and quickly locate dependent objects.

In this section:

- Compacting and repairing your database
- Analyzing your database
- Protecting your data
- Viewing object dependencies

Compacting and repairing your database

As changes are made to your data over a period of time, such as when data is deleted or updated, the data will eventually no longer be ordered on the physical storage in the most efficient manner. Over time, as objects are created and removed, the database will also grow in size. Compacting the database reduces the size of the files and makes the database operate faster by reorganizing the physical data. Before you can compact or repair a shared database, you must ensure that no one is using it.

The repair operation corrects for any problems in the consistency of the data or indexes in the database. A single process is used to both compact and repair a database.

Compact and repair a database

1 With your database open, click the File tab.

2 Click Compact & Repair. This will compact and repair the database and will reopen the database when the process is completed.

3 Drag your database onto the desktop to create a shortcut.

(continued on the next page)

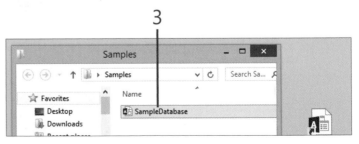

> **TIP** To create a shortcut, click to select the database, hold down the right mouse button, drag the file to for example the desktop, release the mouse button and select Create shortcuts here.

Compact and repair a database *(continued)*

4 Right-click the shortcut, select Properties, and then edit the target by entering a space followed by **/Compact**.

5 Click OK. This creates a shortcut that you can click to compact and repair your database.

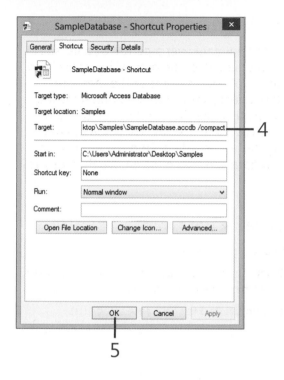

4

5

✓ **TIP** You can use the File tab Options submenu and select the Current Database choice, where an option is provide to Compact on Close which when set means that every time you close the database it will automatically be compacted and repaired.

Analyzing your database

Access provides the following tools for gaining an overview of your database structure:

- The Documenter tool provides you with a basic level of documentation on your design.

- The Analyze Performance tool looks at the structure of your database and provides recommendations for revisions that you can make to the design of the database.

- The Analyze Table tool can restructure tables to provide for a more flexible and relational structure.

Document a database

1 Click the Database Tools tab.

2 Click Database Documenter.

3 Use the tabs and check boxes in the Documenter popup window to select objects that you want to document.

4 Click OK to produce a report documenting the selected objects.

> ✓ **TIP** The default documentation can produce a large amount of paper. One of the available options enables you to produce a shorter summary of the information.

Analyze performance of a database

1 Click the Database Tools tab.

2 Click Analyze Performance.

3 In the Performance Analyzer popup window, use the tabs and check boxes to select objects to analyze.

4 Click OK to receive advice about improving performance of your database.

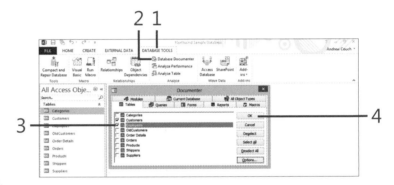

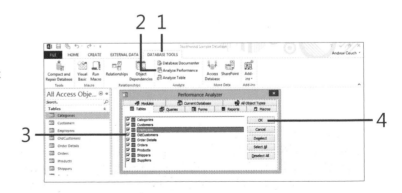

Analyze a table

1 Click the Database Tools tab.

2 Click Analyze Table.

3 Follow the instructions in the Table Analyzer Wizard to analyze the design of a table.

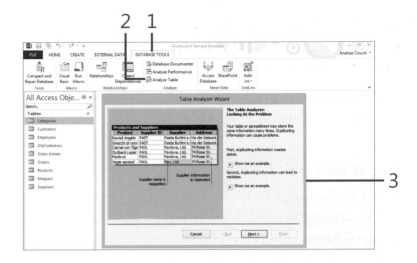

SEE ALSO If you need to manually undertake these operations, then in Section 7 "Modifying data using queries" we show how to create new tables for your data based on existing tables, and in Section 4 "Creating a desktop database" we described how to add relationships between any new tables.

Protecting your data

A database can be protected with a password. This prevents unauthorized users from successfully opening the database. As part of the password protection process, the database is encrypted to prevent other software tools from being used to examine the data.

To add or remove a password, you must access the database by using a special sequence of steps that will open the database with the Open Exclusive option.

Protect a database

1 Click the File tab, and select Open.

2 Select the file location.

3 Browse to locate the file.

4 In the Open popup window, select the file.

5 Change the option to Open Exclusive.

(continued on the next page)

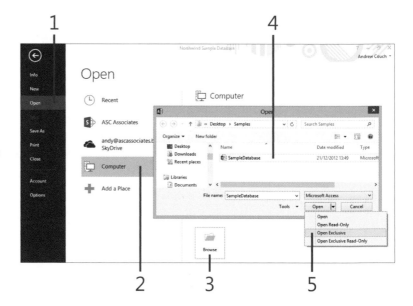

Protect a database *(continued)*

6 After the database opens, return to the File menu, and click Encrypt With Password.

7 Type a password, type it again to verify it, and click OK.

8 Click OK on the warning message indicating that row-level locking will be ignored.

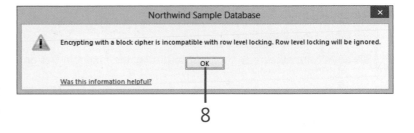

> ✓ **TIP** To remove a database password, repeat these steps for the database. At step 6, the icon will be labeled Decrypt Database. To decrypt the database, you need to have opened the database for exclusive use.

> ✓ **TIP** The warning displayed in step 8 means that although Access is designed to allow multiple users to share data, because you have chosen to further constrain the sharing of data with encryption Access can no longer share data out to other users with the normal flexibility of locking individual rows, it will lock pages of data. This is not normally a serious limitation in a database with few users. In a database which was shared out to a larger number of users you would probably not want to impose encryption because encryption reduces performance and in addition, offers less flexibility in the method of locking data.

Viewing object dependencies

The database has an internal map that tells Access where an object like a table is used in queries, in relationships to other tables, and on forms and reports. This feature enables the product to automatically modify the design of dependent objects when you make changes in an object.

For example, say you have a table with a field called [Contact Name], and you decide to remove the space and rename it [ContactName].

Now imagine that you have queries, forms, and reports that all refer to [Contact Name]. However, because Access has a map of the dependencies, it can automatically correct references to [Contact Name]. Note that there are some limitations on these changes, relating to using the object name in more complex expressions and calculations.

View an object's dependencies

1 Select an object in the navigation pane.

2 Click the Database Tools tab.

3 Click Object Dependencies.

4 Click any of the objects on the right to display the object in Design view.

5 Close the Object Dependencies pane, and open a table in Design view. Then click Object Dependencies to see how this feature can be activated when you have a table in Design view.

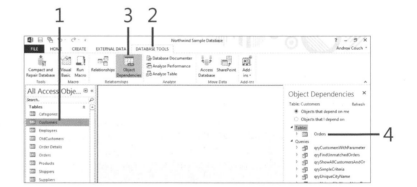

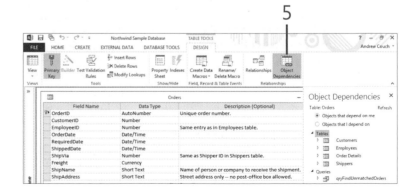

Index

About the Author

Andrew Couch has been working with Microsoft Access since 1992 as a developer, trainer, and consultant. He is a joint founder of the UK Access User Group and has been a Microsoft Access MVP for the past six years. He is the author of *Microsoft Access 2010 VBA Programming Inside Out*, and he is a co-author of *Microsoft Office Professional 2013 Step by Step*. Andrew also provides free technical articles for Access at *www.upsizing.co.uk/TechLibrary.aspx*.

What do you think of this book?

We want to hear from you!

To participate in a brief online survey, please visit:

microsoft.com/learning/booksurvey

Tell us how well this book meets your needs—what works effectively, and what we can do better. Your feedback will help us continually improve our books and learning resources for you.

Thank you in advance for your input!